Josiah Royce

THE OKLAHOMA WESTERN BIOGRAPHIES
RICHARD W. ETULAIN, GENERAL EDITOR

Josiah Royce in his maturity. About 1914—pioneer in the golden age of American philosophy, champion of community and loyalty, child of the American West. (Courtesy of the Department of Special Collections, University Research Library, UCLA)

Josiah Royce

FROM GRASS VALLEY TO HARVARD

By Robert V. Hine

UNIVERSITY OF OKLAHOMA PRESS : NORMAN AND LONDON

by Robert V. Hine

California's Utopian Colonies (San Marino, 1953; New Haven, 1966; New York, 1973; Berkeley, 1983)

(editor) *William Andrew Spalding, Los Angeles Newspaperman: An Autobiographical Account* (San Marino, 1961)

Edward Kern and American Expansion (New Haven, 1962), reissued as *In the Shadow of Frémont: Edward Kern and the Art of American Exploration, 1845–1860* (Norman, 1982)

(editor) *The Irvine Ranch,* by Robert Glass Cleland (San Marino, 1962) (editor, with Edwin R. Bingham) *The Frontier Experience: Readings in the Trans-Mississippi West* (Belmont, 1963)

Bartlett's West: Drawing the Mexican Boundary (New Haven, 1968)

(editor, with Edwin R. Bingham) *The American Frontier: Readings and Documents* (Boston, 1972)

(editor, with Savoie Lottinville) *Soldier in the West: Letters of Theodore Talbot During His Services in California, Mexico, and Oregon, 1845–1853* (Norman, 1972)

The American West: An Interpretive History (Boston, 1973, 1984)

Community on the American Frontier: Separate but Not Alone (Norman, 1980)

California Utopianism: Contemplations of Eden (San Francisco, 1981)

Josiah Royce: From Grass Valley to Harvard (Norman, 1992)

Libary of Congress Cataloging-in-Publication Data

Hine, Robert V., 1921–
    Josiah Royce: from Grass Valley to Harvard / by Robert V. Hine.
        p.   cm. — (Oklahoma western biographies ; v. 4)
    Includes bibliographical references and index.
    ISBN 0-8061-2375-3
    1. Royce, Josiah, 1855–1916. 2. Philosophers—United States—
    Biography. I. Title. II. Series.
    B945.R64H56   1991
    191—dc20
    [B]   91-25613
                                                                              CIP

Josiah Royce: From Grass Valley to Harvard is Volume 4 in *The Oklahoma Western Biographies.*

The paper in this book meets the guidelines for permanence and durability of the Committee on Production Guidelines for Book Longevity of the Council on Library Resources, Inc.(∞)

Royce invoked the spirit of "all those faithful lovers of wounded and shattered communities." To them, the cooperative idealists of the world, who have nourished the beloved community on countless fragmented frontiers, I dedicate this work.

Contents

Illustrations

Series Editor's Preface

IN this sprightly biography of philosopher Josiah Royce, Robert V. Hine chronicles the life of a notable westerner and leading American intellectual of the late-nineteenth and early-twentieth centuries. Balancing and blending elements of Royce's life story, cultural background, and intellectual milieu, the author spins the engrossing story of an intellectual Huckleberry Finn, spiraling outward from the image of a shy, village boy in a remote frontier mining town to that of a world-renowned philosopher at Harvard University.

Hine supplies an especially full account of Royce's western years. Removed from the guiding hand of a strong, ever-present father, young Josiah instead matured under the direction of his ambitious, energetic mother and his older, adoring sisters. Particularly sensitive to the socio-cultural life of Royce's boyhood and adolescent years in Grass Valley and the Bay Area, Hine marshals numerous vivid sensory details to depict Royce's early years in rural and urban California. Gradually freeing himself from his mother's devout Evangelicalism—but not from her dreams for his education—Josiah became a young intellectual in his high-school and University of California years. A year of study in Germany, a Ph.D. at Johns Hopkins, his first years of college teaching at the University of California, and increasing contacts with leading scholars helped Royce land a coveted position in Harvard's Philosophy Department. Although Royce lived the remainder of his life in Cambridge, Massachusetts, the West remained strongly in his mind, in the history and fiction he wrote about California and in the western metaphors and expressions that spiced his popular and scholarly philosophical writings.

In addition to placing Josiah Royce in regional, national, and historical cultural-intellectual contexts, Hine challenges popular stereotypes that reduce the frontier to a Wild West. True, the frontier produced or encouraged such lively figures as Buffalo Bill Cody, Billy the Kid, and Calamity Jane; but in Royce's time it also spawned or nurtured such nationally significant cultural and intellectual figures as Samuel Clemens, Henry George, Abigail Scott Duniway, Jack London, William Randolph Hearst, and Willa Cather. In short, Hine's study of Josiah Royce illustrates a diverse, complicated West too often missing in popular fiction, film, and myths dramatizing the Old West.

Robert Hine, then, has achieved the two major goals of volumes in the Oklahoma Western Biographies series: he has told the appealing life story of Josiah Royce—a young western man who developed into an internationally recognized philosopher—and he has limned the geographical, cultural, and intellectual milieus that influenced Royce's life. Following volumes on George Armstrong Custer, Juan de Oñate, and Narcissa Whitman, this biography further illustrates the challenging complexities of the history and culture of the American West.

RICHARD W. ETULAIN

University of New Mexico

Preface

WHEN a boy is raised in an American frontier mining town and grows to maturity as one of his nation's leading intellectuals, two questions might surface. First, what did his childhood mean to his later life? What was "the landscape of a western mind," as the novelist Ivan Doig would phrase it; how can we feel "into these oldest shadows for the first sudden edge of it all"? Second, what has his life to say about the nature of the western experience? Here is the question of the cultural landscape itself, the way we look upon the environment that produced the mind and personality. This book follows both these trails. It assumes that the West was, as the historian Howard Lamar once said, "inspirer and liberator of the mind as well as of the person." In short, the West, more than rough-and-tumble action, was also thought and emotion. Hence Doig and Lamar prefigure my two goals: tracing the landscape of a western intellect, however far it might be transplanted, and thereby expanding our view of the western experience.

"If one were to write the 'forbidden' biography of Josiah Royce, a narrative of his California period would form one of its most interesting chapters." So wrote a Royce student and distinguished philosopher, who knew his master well. Until Kevin Starr's writing on Royce and John Clendenning's biography, that narrative has been, not so much forbidden, as stymied by the absence of personal papers. Happily, supplementing Clendenning, an additional body of Royce family letters and documents was obtained in the summer of 1989 by the Harvard Archives. They have added substantially to the human side of the story.

We should recognize, however, that Royce himself did not have much use for biography. "The tea-pot ocean of anecdote," he called it. "Would you know the man," as his sister paraphrased him, "read his message"—go to his books, his works; resist rummaging in the details of his childhood. The individual, said Royce, is so precious, so unique, that he is "incapable of being explained through any knowledge of his heredity, or of his environment, or of anything which is not himself."

George Santayana, Wolfgang Amadeus Mozart, and Charles Sanders Peirce, it is said, "each produced voluminous work, but each finally concealed himself within it." Royce fits in that company. It is not easy to find the man in his philosophical work. Perhaps that is one unwitting meaning behind a western youngster's fan letter to the mature Royce: "Why don't you write a funny book?" In other words, why don't you reveal more sides of yourself. Josiah Royce was no Mark Twain. Yet I contend that within his serious writings and philosophy one can find his western roots. In short, I propose to do for Royce what Royce once proposed to do for Percy Shelley: "to consider his place in the great mountain chain or range of his age, an age as full of great and small things, of beautiful and of terrible things, as ever were Ural Mountains or Sierra, Andes or Himalaya." Buried in these metaphors of great, beautiful, and terrible things are the Sierra Nevada, the cradle of his western soul. They and San Francisco and Berkeley are his nucleus from and around which an erudite life and a grand philosophy emerged and revolved. Yet this is not a book of philosophy; even chapter 8 can be conveniently omitted by readers not philosophically inclined. The permutations of Royce's idealism are treated too well elsewhere. Rather the book proceeds from a simple premise, that this wonderful man's life and thought moved in ever-widening concentric circles, that the end was in the beginning.

Among those gyrating circles were mathematics and science and, above all, a love of literature that the man carried from childhood. The epigraphs for the following chapters suggest that latter love. When not in his own words, they are drawn from the romantic poets and nineteenth-century novelists that he revered. Goethe, Wordsworth, Byron, Browning, and George Eliot were authors he read as a boy in Grass Valley and San Francisco; they remained inspirations throughout his life.

This study has utilized primary and archival as well as secondary materials, but the canons of the series outlaw footnotes. Therefore, I have placed a fully annotated copy of the manuscript in the Tomás Rivera Library of the University of California, Riverside, California 92521. It is available on request through Interlibrary Loan.

The editors of the *Pacific Historical Review* and the *California Historical Quarterly* have graciously granted permission to reprint in revised form two portions of work that they previously published.

The staffs of the following institutions have once again won my heart and my sincere thanks: the Huntington Library, San Marino, California; the Harvard Archives in the Pusey Library; the Bancroft Library of the University of California, Berkeley; Special Collections, Library of the University of California, Los Angeles; and especially the Tomás Rivera Library of the University of California, Riverside.

John Clendenning and Frank Oppenheim (who along with Bruce Kuklick and Kevin Starr are the leading scholars of Royce) have been to me wonderfully friendly and helpful. All historians mine one another, but I have capitalized on the generosity of these two men far beyond the usual. Their published works were incomparable guides; their words and letters were rich with answers and clues. In a similarly important way Nancy A. Hacker became an invaluable resource on Royce family history.

The editor of the series, Richard Etulain, was a warm support through all stages. Likewise, I sincerely thank the editors of the University of Oklahoma Press, John Drayton and Sarah Nestor. Aimee Myers carefully read and checked the manuscript; without her it would have been a great deal poorer.

The many others who have helped in this book are listed below in alphabetical order. My appreciation for their contributions is invariably heartfelt. The totality of my indebtedness is like the Great Plains to the wheat seed, beyond enormity. I thank Tony Bliss, Peter Blodgett, James T. Brown, David Breninger, Robert Chandler, Julia Child, Walter Conser, John Mack Faragher, Peter Fuss, Edwin S. Gaustad, Mary Gazlay, Donn Headley, Oliver A. Johnson, Bruce Kuklick, Christopher Lasch, Patricia Nelson Limerick, Elizabeth Lopez, Lou Masur, David Moore, Irene Moran, June O'Connor, Earl Pomeroy, Martin Ridge, William Roberts, Eric Rood, Josiah Royce III, Albert Shumate, Sarah Stage, William Sturm, Ruth Sutter, Ed Tyson, Martha Winnacker, and Robert Wyckoff.

Royce once compared a man without loyalty to a stranded ship with torn canvas still flapping in the wind. Without Shirley I could be that same ship, and this manuscript could still be breezily fluttering.

Robert V. Hine

Josiah Royce

CHAPTER I

Pioneer Pilgrims

There are wanderers o'er Eternity
Whose bark drives on and on,
        and anchor'd ne'er shall be.
        Byron, *Childe Harold's Pilgrimage*

SARAH Eleanor Bayliss Royce was the epitome of a woman whose pioneering life intensified rather than relaxed her deepest moral commitments. She clutched her values around her and set forth to survive. Through her stubborn will, her Protestant culture thrived on the frontier. She carried both the will and the culture all the way from Stratford-on-Avon in England, where she was born. Her father, a tailor, brought her to America as a baby of three months along with five older brothers and sisters. They lived in Germantown, Pennsylvania, and New York City until, when she was nine, the family moved to Rochester, New York.

In cold and leafy upstate New York, she learned stamina, enough to carry her through her western ordeals. And her English parents saw that she was educated, too, as extensively as a woman then could be, with an "old-style academy education." So her daughter-in-law phrased it, but Sarah's education was actually more impressive than that. She graduated from the Phipps Union Female Seminary of Albion, New York, where she studied the liberal arts along with etiquette, housewifery, and religion. She never stopped learning, for her reading, especially in religion, endowed her life. Following graduation, she taught school, as she would at many other times in her life. Later, on the overland trail, faced with the need to jettison belongings, she never forsook her basic books—her

Bible and her copy of John Milton. In the Great Basin desert when once rummaging through a cache of valuables abandoned by a previous wagon train, Sarah passed over all the portable treasures but one, a book titled *Little Ella*, which she could read to her child.

Sarah Bayliss, who bore a famous son on whom she would exert a commanding influence, herself grew up amid conditions that emulated most frontiers. In the 1830s through a natural funnel formed by the Finger Lakes to the south and the Great Lakes to the north, the Erie Canal traced an unobstructed, easy route from New England to the West. The region channeled the Northeast's mobile energies, flowing into this booming area and then out along the Ohio River toward successive frontiers. Free of their traditional religious restraints, transient New Englanders and displaced New Yorkers experimented with wave after wave of cultist enthusiasms, such as the Millerite millenialists and the Rochester rapping spiritualists. And more tenacious doctrines, like Mormonism and Seventh-Day Adventism, grew up in this "burnt-over district." The Bayliss family, with a firm religious base, was probably not tempted, but they must have been aware of these religious fervors; Sarah certainly inherited an evangelical zeal not unlike the religions of that region. But the denomination she eventually called her own was a product of other frontiers.

This was the church of the Disciples of Christ, and it came out of frontier Kentucky's Cane Ridge revival in 1804. Its original branch hoped to restore Christianity to primal ways by preaching the gospel "without any mixture of philosophy, vain deceit, traditions of men, or the rudiments of the world." Five years later in western Pennsylvania Alexander Campbell called for a similar restoration of the primitive church as a means of unifying the "many broils, dissensions, and anathemas" of Christianity. In time united, these two groups formed the Disciples of Christ, sometimes called simply the Christian Church. Sarah Bayliss found its doctrines compelling.

In Josiah Royce, Sr., Sarah met a man who was her equal in

religious commitment. He, too, was born an Englishman in a Midlands village east of Leicester. His family brought him to New York at the age of four and then on to the Canadian rim of Lake Ontario. There the family helped found the Baptist Church of Dundas, and Josiah, "while still quite young," was immersed and united with the society of the Baptists. "From very early youth," according to his eventual obituary, "Mr. Royce showed much interest in religious reading and conversation." Sometime in his late teens he moved to Rochester, where he first encountered Sarah, the young teacher. Quite likely they met at religious meetings.

Josiah Royce and Sarah Bayliss were married on the last day of May 1845. She was seven years his junior, probably his superior in intellect and will, and a good soul-mate on the Christian pilgrims' progress. Their relationship seemed strong and loving; they bore children regularly. It is possible to infer something of their days together from a description of the husband.

> He began early in life to lay the foundation for that familiarity with scripture which in later life enabled him to recite from memory, passage after passage upon the same subject, beginning often with the earliest prophesies, and adding one quotation after another bearing upon the same point until he ended the book of Revelations.

They lived for three years in Rochester, and there Sarah bore their first daughter, Mary Eleanor. Having a family did not prevent the young father's restlessness. Motion was in his days, as was once said of Daniel Boone, and Josiah trekked with his wife and baby down the Ohio and out to a farming village three miles from Tipton in eastern Iowa. It was most likely a first step in a broader plan to reach California. We do not know whether Sarah desired this move, but a woman of her abilities must have winced at leaving eastern advantages. She loved her place, the river, "my own, old Genesee," she called it. But consoling herself with biblical accounts of the woman in the wilderness, she probably assented dutifully.

Once in Iowa, however, she reconciled herself to moving again within that first year.

Not just religious, Josiah had shown himself to be also a roamer. His wife shared some of that drive. In "laughing girlhood," as she put it, she read of a place called Sutter's Fort in California, and "I used to threaten I would go and see that Fort some day, and stand on the Pacific shore." Within them both, but especially within Josiah, was Stephen Vincent Benét's "loadstone of the iron in the breast, never to be forgotten or possessed." And the year was 1849! Loadstones in the breast were everywhere leaping at the thoughts of gold. Did the husband convince his wife to go? Or, once he decided, did she have to persuade him to take her along? In either case, Sarah was always spunky and never a whiner. "If we were going, let us go, and meet what we were to meet, bravely. So I seated myself in the wagon, my little two-year old Mary was placed beside me, my husband and the other man of our little company started the team, and we were on our way."

So began a journey long to be remembered in the annals of the westward crossing because Sarah so graphically described it in what she called her "Pilgrim's Diary."

> I had for months anticipated this hour, yet, not till it came, did I realize the blank dreariness of seeing night come on without house or home to shelter us and our baby-girl. And this was to be the same for many weeks, perhaps months. It was a chilling prospect, and there was a terrible shrinking from it in my heart; but I kept it all to myself and we were soon busy making things as comfortable as we could for the night.

But that first night she could not sleep from "the oppressive sense of homelessness . . . in one whose life had so far, been spent in city or town, surrounded by the accompaniments of civilization."

Rain and wind and mud claimed seven days before they even got to Iowa City, some thirty miles west of Tipton. Three weeks later at Council Bluffs they found "a city of wagons" waiting to be ferried across the Missouri. It took another week for their turn, but Sarah did not complain. The men, as far as she could see, exhibited the "utmost quiet and good humor." Amid the waiting camps, however, in many a makeshift kitchen enclosure, she found "a feminine heart, yearning for home." Finally across the river on June 8, she said "farewell to the fag-end of civilization on the Atlantic side of the continent."

In her mind Indians were a frightful threat, but death, more imminent, "made our wagon his first point of attack." An old man who had joined them was convulsed with spasms and died shortly of cholera. That night as the wagon was being disinfected, she sat up, her mind on the diseased body stretched on the rude bier outside, its winding sheet flapping in the wind and suggesting "some vindictive creature struggling restlessly in bonds." Beyond, Indians in a flickering light chanted "shrill notes as of distressful appeal. The minor key ran through it all. I knew it was a death dirge."

The strains were not improved as they left Salt Lake, "a solitary wagon, drawn by three yoke of oxen, and in charge of only two men . . . bearing, as its passengers, one woman and one little child." The other man was "considerably advanced in years, and not in perfect health."

Shortly afterward, traveling at night to avoid the heat, this pitiful group overshot a turning where they were to refit. Instead they found themselves next morning on the barren sands with insufficient water and forage, "a forlorn little company wrecked upon the desert." They fed their oxen the pathetic amount of hay in their mattresses and swallowed hard to abate their own thirst. Forward or back, certain death seemed to await. Desperately weary from the night's travel and the morning's debate, they opted for a short noonday nap before a final decision, one way or the other. All slept but Sarah.

With unwearied gaze my eyes swept, again and again, the shimmering horizon. There was no help or hope there. Then I looked at what lay nearest. How short-lived our few remaining resources would be, unless fresh strength came soon from somewhere. How still it was. Only the sound of a few feeble breaths. It would not take many hours of starvation to quiet them forever.

In that moment Sarah showed herself a woman apart.

> Whence came this calm strength which girded me round so surely, while I, and all surrounding me were so weak? I had known what it was to *believe* in God, and to pray that He would never leave us. Was it thus then, that when all other helpers failed, He came so near that I no longer simply *believed* in Him, but *knew* His presence there, giving strength for whatever might come?

The decision was to go back, a bitter choice, prompting Sarah, now trudging alone behind the wagon, to imagine herself as Abraham's rejected wife, Hagar, "in the wilderness walking wearily away from her fainting child among the dried up bushes. . . ." When she confronted another shrub, bursting aflame from a distant sagebrush fire, she felt again the days of Hagar and Ishmael and, now, of Moses: "the illusion of being a wanderer in a far off, old time desert, and myself witnessing a wonderful phenomenon. For a few moments I stood with bowed head worshiping the God of Horeb, and I was strengthened thereby."

By now it was well into October, far too late to be so distant from the Sierra passes. Amid dead animals and abandoned wagons, the Royces seemed "the last, little, feeble, struggling band at the rear of a routed army." The fate of the Donner party a few years earlier must surely have crossed their minds. But salvation intervened in the form of a United States Army relief party (to Sarah sufficient evidence of the hand of Providence). Under the army's tutelage the Royce wagon was abandoned, their belongings packed on animals, and Sarah with the baby placed on a mule with a common Spanish saddle. Never before had she ridden anything but sidesaddle with "all the usual equipments for lady's riding." But, thus adjusted, the party made it with only ten days to spare before the passes were blocked by an unusually stormy winter.

The story is worth detailing for what it tells of Sarah Royce, probably the single most dominant influence on her son's life. Her character was structured around her religious commitment. Actions, behavior—the basic forms were important. The observance of the Sabbath, for example, was crucial enough, even in dangerous Indian country, to let the main body of the train go on while she and her family "held a social meeting for prayer, reading and singing." Peril, of course, is a little thing when one feels "a rich Providence" so near, feels him in the power of the tempest, the winds, and the blowing sands. To her the thought that the relief party "looked Heaven-sent" immediately grew into a "sweetly solemn conviction." It was a simple, Old Testament faith, filled with thoughts of Hagar, Ebenezer, and the Promised Land. Sarah and Josiah, indeed even their names, illuminated how obvious in frontier religion was the nearness of the Deity and how immediate were the messages of the Old Testament.

Sarah was more than a sentimental mystic. There was in her, too, an independent perverseness. She was not overly critical of moments on the trail when every man was "bent for himself," though those moments were often disastrous to their own well-being. "Perverse were we," she said, and she was proud of it, along with being a part of "us old-fashioned people." No mirage tempted Sarah Royce, though along their thirsty path sheets of water and placid rivers lay beckoning. Even alone and frightened, she stared a wild coyote in the eye and dared him to attack. She climbed Independence Rock on the Sweetwater River with only her baby and another woman and considered it "not too rash an undertaking."

Her imagination was vivid, even romantic. She conversed with a lone tree and imagined its old heart being cheered by immigrant voices vibrating among its branches. When she first looked down into the Sacramento Valley, it was into California's "smiling face. I loved you from that moment." But the romanticism was tempered with practicality. She understood clearly that, when it came to Indians, the aim of a pioneer's rifle defined their safety. God was the ultimate comfort, but he was not a substitute for other practical resources.

The father was less of an anchor than the mother. His faith, for example, did not determine the religion of the family, but rather Sarah's. Once in California the Baptist father became a Disciple. Thereafter, however, he was as zealous as his wife, helping found the Christian Church of Grass Valley and serving as its trustee. He provided, however, only a minimum of stability. Some drifting qualities seemed innate in his character, but more important, he was the victim of circumstances. Many otherwise stable men were undermined by the gold rush, tempted beyond endurance by a restless society and economic adversity. Journalists of more settled mining towns, such as Grass Valley, worried over those who moved on instead of staying and building. One of Grass Valley's earliest miners, Samuel Nichols, wrote home, "There are a great many stories, and very strange ones, too, got up for the purpose of an excitement in this new country." Even men like John Coad, a Grass Valley Cornishman who had ridiculed other miners for always seeking riches elsewhere, succumbed himself in the winter of 1859 and set off for the snows of British Columbia.

Such a society the Royces entered in October 1849. It would take five years before they found Grass Valley. Their first stop of only two months was a settlement that Sarah remembered as Weaverville, better known as Weberville or Webertown, two or three miles above Placerville. Their first camp was a measure of their desperation and their luck.

Gold-rush California in many ways would blindly determine their married lives. At the same time, the emerging society would itself be shaped by the character and resolve of people like themselves. The two forces of luck and character seemed to act quite differently on Sarah and Josiah.

For him, luck did not smile, at least not in fortune. To begin with, he lost two mules, one of his own and a black mule, one of the two the army relief party lent them in the mountains. The army animal with fifteen feet of rope on its neck took off toward Sacramento, and as far as we know, Royce never saw it again. He wrote apologetically to John Chandler, mule handler at the fort in Sacramento (not a captain, as Royce addressed him), that he was "grieved to think that you should sustain any loss on our account," and that he would "continue to hunt the woods for mules in this section." If Royce had come to California to pan for gold, we have no record of his ever finding any. If he had come to make a merchant fortune, it eluded him. If he had come to find good land to settle and claim for himself and his children, he was frustrated. The army mule was an augury.

Sarah, however, either courted success or was of a disposition to make a success of whatever she found. In their Weaverville tent, she was intelligent enough to be aware of the dangers of robbery or, perhaps worse, that "some impertinent person might so easily intrude, or hang about, in a troublesome manner." But, sewing inside the canvas walls, she overheard rough woodcutters acting like gentlemen, warning one another to be careful lest a stray stick hit the woman and child within. Instead of impertinent persons, Sarah met very different types: a former lawyer, a scientist, and a young physician seeking "means of support for his widowed mother and the younger members of his family." The only other woman in town, probably a prostitute, visited Sarah in "a new gown with full trimmings" and asked her to a dance. Sarah politely refused, but in her telling of the story, the prostitute was only a cook for the publican's boarders. Something in Sarah kept her head high and her eyes above the dust of the road.

"On all sides the gold-pans were rattling, the cradles rocking, and the water splashing," she wrote. Josiah found two partners, raised adjacent tents for a house and store, and installed counter and shelves in the front one and a cookstove in the rear. Sarah served the motley customers and learned to weigh gold dust in little scales. She listened to the complaints and discontents of the miners but blamed them for their chronic chase after new discoveries, which "kept the whole community in a ferment."

Bad luck, continuing to frown, brought down this initial enterprise. Cholera struck both the husband and his wife, and when Sarah was still weak from her bout, Josiah decided to get out. He put her in a wagonbed and her child in a seat beside her, heaped on their belongings, and a few days after Christmas took off down the mountains to Sacramento.

Disappointment followed. In a city which had grown in that one year from a camp to a town of ten thousand, Royce and his partners had managed to build a wood floor under a tent to be their house and store, but the floods of that January washed them out. Sarah, only barely recovered from her cholera, camped with her child in the unfinished upstairs room of a pioneering surgeon. The waters swirled for days below, and the men came back and forth by boat. Eventually the family boarded the steamer *McKim* and plowed through miles of muddy waters by hordes of shivering, huddled refugees, noting only one woman and child among the many men. On January 16 they anchored in San Francisco at the foot of Telegraph Hill, the sun bright on its grassy slopes.

There was no housing for them in San Francisco in the winter of 1850. While Josiah scoured the town, day after day, Sarah and Mary Eleanor roomed at the Montgomery House on Montgomery Street between California and Pine in a narrow double-bunk room with no furniture. During the long rainy days she took her child to sit by the only stove, which happened to be in the barroom. Though the men were "far from refined in manners," she witnessed (or chose to witness) "no rough or discourteous word" and "no offensive behavior." Sarah lived in an armor that insulated her from much of the world.

Yet a sturdy practicality sustained her as well. She was always willing to take what came. A newly arrived Protestant minister told them of an uncompleted apartment in a building he was occupying. The apartment as yet had only one inhabitable room, but Sarah was game, especially since they could use the minister's quarters when necessary. For that reason she now felt with renewed passion "the brightness of the evening lamp-light" and "the cheeriness of the morning breakfast room, with all their orderly accompaniments." Her voice was the remembered East wrestling with a rough foreign world.

"I had never before realized the worth of quiet domestic life, unworried by ever-threatening dangers."

The house of "tenements," though it was constructed only of paper and cloth, turned out to be a unified fortress of communal respectability. The residents included at least five families, perhaps more, "true to their convictions, earnest in their religious life, and faithful and lovely in the domestic circle." During the thirteen months the Royces lived there, this group of families shared one wedding, one death, and two child-births—one of which in July 1850 was Sarah's, their second daughter, Harriette. Together they "gazed with terror" on the fire of May 4, 1850, and expressed their fears as cholera stalked the city. It was the kind of group that rejoiced at the rise of new churches and the beginnings of religious newspapers. And they felt particular relief when California became a part of their old homeland, as on that October day they watched through a spyglass the arrival of the *Oregon* with its message of admission to the union.

Sometime in the winter of 1850–51 they were off again, this time to the Contra Costa shores of the bay near Martinez. Overlooking the Carquinez Straits, where the interior rivers and Suisun Bay merge into the San Pablo arm of the larger bay, Sarah called it "one of the most beautifully located villages, that the steamboat traveler of those early days admired, as he journied from the metropolis to the interior," thinking of the packets from San Francisco to Sacramento. By 1851 a new stone jailhouse in Martinez stood not far from the wharf. Two women had already opened schools in their houses.

Sarah was supremely happy on their inland farm, glorying in the spring flowers or the golden hills under ever-green oaks and gigantic madronas while her children played along El Hambre Creek. She felt again "the constant presence of the great and good One, her own Helper and Friend." Here in August 1852 she bore a son, John Samuel, but the baby died shortly after birth. There was yet no church, but members of four different denominations met in the schoolhouse to hear visiting preachers and conduct a little Sunday school.

On that East Bay farm they lived over two years through the special census of September 1852 and until the spring of 1853. Sarah reminisced, "There was then granted to me an extra installment of youth; so unexpectedly rich and fresh were the experiences that came to me during that time."

Her husband, however, was not doing too well. He was active enough in the community, signing a petition to the state legislature in February 1851 against a bill that would change the laws on divorce and another in March to charter a ferry between Martinez and Benicia. Financial problems, however, crowded around him. On January 20, 1852, he with a man named Babcock gave a note to one Richard C. Swain for $170 "for value received" at 5 percent interest per month. In May Swain sued for the money, then totaling $210.16. Property was attached (two of Royce's mules with harness and wagon), and in the courthouse, meeting then in the upstairs of the Berryessa adobe residence, there were summons and surety bonds and appeals. The appeal was withdrawn by Royce in July; by then he had either paid the debt or forfeited his mules and wagon. Just before they left Martinez, Royce was sued again, for $247.52.

So the family moved as so often before. Some women might have rebelled at being uprooted once more and being carted off to another mining camp, but we have no record of Sarah complaining. This time she and Josiah ended in a mining town on a river about twenty miles from Sacramento. It was probably in the neighborhood of Mississippi Bar or Texas Hill, though it may have been at Beals Bar, where an intention to build a ditch is recorded on September 28, 1852. Josiah had apparently heard of a big hydraulic venture being constructed with a dam, a steam engine, and a great flume. It was attracting its share of miners, and a jerry-built town was springing up. The Royces found an enclosed spot on the bluff under three young oaks and raised a frame house covered with cloth. Sarah did her best. She carpeted the floor with matting, curtained off a corner for the bedroom, stood up the trunks for furniture, set up boxes for cupboards around the cookstove, stuffed and covered other boxes for "ottomans," and installed in the "parlor" the pride of her life, her melodeon. "At night when, the children were all in bed . . . I used often to indulge myself in the melodies and harmonies that brought to me the most precious memories of earth, and opened up visions of heaven. And then those bare rafters, and cloth walls became for the time a banquet-hall, a cathedral."

But the economy was less harmonious. The miners objected to the water rates. There were stormy meetings and wild speeches. The San Francisco capitalists refused to budge and, instead of lowering rates, closed the flume. In a few months the Royces were on the road again.

The plan now was to homestead land some distance out of a flourishing mining town on the main road from Sacramento to the mountains, very likely Folsom. Here, because it was summer (1853), they built an outdoor kitchen and eating area under a tarp and hung cupboards from the trees. This left their framed cloth house, which they disassembled and reconstructed, to be a grander bedroom and parlor. From it the melodeon soon echoed across the hills.

With Josiah working in town, Sarah was often alone with the children, and she suffered several frights from rough men along the Sacramento road. So that autumn of 1853 they moved into town. The move was associated with the birth of another baby, the third daughter, Ruth, on September 21, 1853. There were few families in that society of single males, but among them were those who liked to drop by the Royces' frame cottage and sing around the melodeon. Outside the bachelor miners made fun of their "psalm singing." Yet when the Royces offered their parlor to a visiting preacher, the room was packed.

This stay was only for the winter. During these first five years since they descended the mountains on relief mules, Sarah set up housekeeping in eight new places, counting the Montgomery House. There were no gold strikes, no fine strokes of good fortune. Royce may possibly have saved up a bit of money. At least he had enough to buy land in the next town. This time the new home would bring Sarah over ten years of relative rest. But she could not have predicted such reprise while in the spring of 1854 the band of pilgrims— Josiah and Sarah and their three daughters—tramped through the mud and dust toward Grass Valley.

CHAPTER 2

Grass Valley

Thou best philosopher, who yet dost keep
Thy heritage. . . .
Wordsworth, "Intimations
of Immortality"

JOSIAH and Sarah jolted their wagon into Grass Valley in the spring of 1854 to set up their ninth California abode. They found a town that had grown from under five hundred in 1850 to several thousand, with ten to twelve men for every woman. Up the road about four miles was Nevada City, a twin and rival town; to the west about thirty miles was Marysville, on the Yuba River near its intersection with the Sacramento.

Josiah had undoubtedly heard that Grass Valley was a model of permanence among California's gold-rush towns, because it so early moved from placer to hard-rock mining. Of course, the first gold seekers primitively washed gravel as they camped in the grassy valley along Wolf Creek, but that was in 1849. By the following year the solid, underground, precious quartz of Gold Hill and Ophir Hill lured new forms of technology. The veins of golden ore, unusually thin in the Grass Valley region—in miners' stories as thin as the filling in a bad pie—were cracked out of the solid rock, stamped and pulverized at a mill, and melted into bricks. Though the first stamping was done with capped logs, almost as rudimentary as a Mexican *arrastra*, iron stamps were soon introduced, and large mechanized operations followed. Grass Valley also pioneered the chlorination process of separating ores. Though that technique succeeded, other experiments failed. Dozens of mines succumbed. But enough held on to give Grass Valley an illusion of stability among the restless mines. The equilibrium,

Grass Valley in 1858. Typical of such promotional materials, the wild qualities of the Grass Valley surroundings are minimized in this contemporary lithograph. Wolf Creek is only vaguely discernible running from lower left to midcenter, and the surrounding hills and woods do not stand out, but the cluster of buildings in the left center includes the Royce house and orchard at Mill and Neal streets. (Courtesy of the Huntington Library, San Marino, California).

however, was not that of a typical American small town, for Grass Valley increasingly included an abnormally large industrial work force shaped by a high percentage of Cornishmen, refugees from the English tin mines. Led by Alonzo Delano, banker and Wells Fargo agent, efforts were afoot to make the community morally and socially respectable.

The Royces rode into a countryside that was heavily broken, each ridge saw-toothed with pines against the sky. Within a few hundred yards of town were woods of black oak and sugar maple mixed with the ponderosa. Grass Valley, where the trees had been largely cut, lay on rising ground to the west of Wolf Creek. Mill Street paralleled the stream and ran from Main Street, the new center of business, to the older settlement at Boston Ravine a short mile to the south. In 1854 there were a few hundred buildings in the town. The houses were generally ramshackle of raw shakes or wood and canvas, but some of the mine owners had built two-story Victorian residences with picket fences, and many of the businesses were already of brick.

Josiah bought land at Mill and Neal streets, between the newer mercantile center and the older Boston Ravine. The parcel, roughly two hundred by two hundred feet, sloped gently from the corner of Neal Street down to Wolf Creek below. Royce erected a small one-story house that his daughter later recalled as "not well built." He planted an orchard, most likely apples and pears, and set up his business, selling and peddling fruit. For Josiah the situation augured well. He combined his production and distribution in one place, an advantage he had sought near Folsom.

From her house Sarah walked with her young children up the one long curving city block of Mill Street to the center of town. Plank sidewalks ran sporadically along Mill and Main. Elsewhere, including their corner, it was mud and dust. Cows and pigs were free to roam the streets. She passed Denman's carriage shop, a smithy, and the fireproof building where McLaughlin sold hardware and stoves. The route included a boot and shoe store and Edwards Bakery and Provision store, on the second floor of which hung the shingle of F. W. Thayer, the attorney. A physician-surgeon and a dentist also practiced in the block. Where Mill deadended into Main Street stood the brick building of Marshall and Company, which sold provisions, liquor, hardware, mining tools, paints, and glass. Depending on which direction she turned on Main Street, she went by the Wells Fargo office, the post office, the town's two hotels (the Beatty House and the Aurora House), or the office of the weekly *Telegraph*. Adjacent to the newspaper office was Stiles Book and Music Emporium. Main Street also included two other shoe stores, a bakery, and a tailor. Taverns and saloons interspersed them all, and we can imagine Sarah urging her children to step by them more quickly.

Within a year Sarah was pregnant for the fifth time. The carrying days were filled with new hopes, economic fears, and at least one severe fright. Seven months into her term, in September 1855, she and her family witnessed Grass Valley's most devastating fire. It burned all night and consumed three hundred buildings, the entire central town. A young sawmill worker, William Shepard, wrote home, "Oh! Oh! O such a fire! such a fire!! Grass Valley went up last night soul, body and breeches . . . clearing off about 30 acres of land in very little time . . . every hotel and tavern was burned. The churches were all saved being out of the limits of the business portion of the town and where the buildings are quite scattering." That sparser area was where the Royces lived, but their house was barely spared. The experience would have been terrifying, especially for a pregnant woman.

Then and later the family, like the residents of similar towns, lived in nearly constant fear of fire. Volunteer fire companies rose but, because of the instability of the population, soon evaporated. Equipment was rare, and when a fire engine was delivered to any of the towns in the area, usually by water to Marysville, it was driven up the valley like a circus chariot and gawked at in every mining camp on its way.

In the house on Mill Street on November 20, 1855, Sarah Royce bore their first surviving son, and they named the child for his father, Josiah. The family was now six: Josiah and Sarah; Mary Eleanor, almost nine; five-year-old Harriette (called Hattie); Ruth, who had just turned two; and now Josiah, Jr., whom the family nicknamed Josie. Someday many would call him America's greatest philosopher, the golden age of American philosophy would rest upon his shoulders, and his watchword would be "community."

During his eleven years in or near Grass Valley, Josie grew into a precocious, left-handed lad with blue eyes and bright red hair. As his sister remembered, he "played much alone and *thought* as he played"; "he did not feel the need of boy companionship." The lonely tendency—the product of temperament, his mother's direction, and the sparcity of the town's children—was not helped by the increasing absence of his father, away on business, seldom at home. The loneliness undoubtedly aided the precocity. Sarah said that "as a child he had been forward in numbers, doing large sums in his head." His forwardness was so obvious to her that sometimes she connived to keep books of arithmetic from him. Shortly after leaving Grass Valley, the boy was doing solid geometry and trigonometry.

Though his mother was the model and companion, the teacher, the law, and the teller of tales from her own overland experience, it was also she who led him through his first exposure to a frontier town. She must have tried to shield him, as hard as that was. Even if she walked with him, street scenes and events entered the mind. The society affected them both, particularly through its unsettledness—only comparatively stable, generally thriving, but nevertheless given to years of depression following the booms.

The people of a mining community appeared on the streets as a polyglot group, hard-rock miners in their twenties, varicolored, largely Cornish, but also Irish and Hispanic and Chinese. To his brother at home, William Shepard described the people of Grass Valley: "plenty of all kinds of the good, bad and indifferent, white, black and brown and other colors—long haired, short haired—and no hair at all." By the

Josiah at five. The earliest known picture. There is little of the roughness of Grass Valley here. Rather, the child already shows a thoughtful bearing. The uniform suggests discipline; the lace ruffle, a mother's hand. (Courtesy of the Harvard University Archives)

time the Royces came, the early romanticizing of the cosmopolitan population was over; Hispanics, for example, were widely seen as vicious in character, suitable chiefly for bordellos and saloons. Their bullfights, it was felt, made it clear how much California needed Americanizing. Know-Nothing sentiment was also directed against the Catholic Irish. The Cornish, however, mixed rather easily with the other Anglo citizenry. For Josie, however, all foreigners stood in the background, never really close to him.

The town was already color segregated. Shepard wrote of going to church, "the front seats reserved for white folks and the back for negros." There was a separate African Methodist Episcopal Church since the year the Royces arrived in town. Many of its members were recent slaves from a nearby mine, the death of whose Georgia owner left them free. The newspaper extolled those blacks who respectfully kept their place. They were not allowed to live in white neighborhoods, however, and when black children in 1855 tried to attend the public school, they were expelled. The Royces reacted to such racial matters, for on February 19, 1858, Josiah followed his propensity for signing petitions, this time to the legislature supporting a law that would allow Negro testimony in court cases involving Caucasians.

Similarly in the background was the demimonde of the gold rush. Lola Montez, known as the mistress of kings, now reduced to honky-tonk entertaining, lived a stone's throw from Josie's birthplace, and when this red-haired boy grew up, his life became so steeped in learning, so filled with erudition, that it came to seem surprising that he was born the neighbor of Lola Montez. Lola actually left town a few months after the boy's birth, but Lola's young protegé, Lotta Crabtree, lived in the same block. It is unlikely that the mother ever let the boy near such brazen women, knowing how many peripatetic miners they enchanted, dancing in their spiderwebs and tantalizing attire. Yet the world of Lola Montez and Lotta Crabtree was a part of Josie's immediate (if not experiential) environment.

By all accounts a boy on the frontier, especially the mining frontier, heard monumental profanity. J. Ross Browne had traveled widely and also knew California mining towns well; he said the cursing of other areas was like "a murmuring brook" compared with "the volume and rush and thunder of a cataract" in Grass Valley. The same was true for all manner of gambling, and prostitution was hard to hide. Yet young Josie, as far as we know, seemed unscarred. His mother successfully guided him through the vices and temptations of Vanity Fair, the Delectable Mountains, and the City of Destruction.

Economic survival, however, was no easier for the Royce family in Grass Valley than it was in previous mining towns. With the inflated economy one income was not enough. Two out of five of the white women in Grass Valley took in boarders to help ends meet. Within a few months of their arrival, Sarah determined to make a similar contribution, but in her case it was to teach school. Sarah enjoyed her own talents, and besides, boarders would upset the sanctity of the home she wanted so much to nurture in this rough society.

In October 1854, before Josie was born, Sarah advertised in the *Telegraph* that she would open that month a school for young ladies. "Mrs. Royce," the announcement went on, "hopes her combined experience as TEACHER AND PARENT may enable her to render her School worthy the support of those who desire a thorough moral and intellectual discipline for their daughters." Boys might be admitted if under the age of ten. There were to be primary, junior, middle, and senior classes, with tuition ranging from four to ten dollars per month. "Rudiments of French" and drawing cost an additional three dollars each. Elocution and vocal music would be taught to all students without charge.

The plan was to open Sarah's school in Mrs. E. P. Goldsmith's rooms at 235 Mill, just down the street by the Montez and Crabtree houses. We can imagine the two women talking of the plans over tea. The following year Mrs. Goldsmith started her own school there, and Sarah moved her pupils to the Royce house. By then she was pregnant with Josie, and home probably seemed more appealing. Mrs. Goldsmith and her husband later projected a competing seminary for young ladies. They put all of the profits from his Lucky Mine into a building, including imported granite and expensive hardwood moldings, but with the foundations and first story completed, the mine gave out, and the seminary remained a crumbling dream, long known in the area as Deacon's Folly.

With so few children Grass Valley established schools slowly. Until 1853 all of the education came through women teaching a few pupils in private. A public school did not open until four years after the camp's beginnings (the year before the Royces arrived) and then barely survived by running frantic campaigns including children's programs before paying parents. As late as 1864 over half the children were taught in private. Sarah's school was in that tradition.

During Josie's early years, Grass Valley noticeably changed from a ramshackle mining camp to something nearer an American village community. By 1855 it was beginning to assign street numbers to its houses and stores in the central part of town. That was a clear sign that merchants were choosing order and stability over the makeshift, "roughing it" life of 1850. A natural disparity grew between the merchants (who numbered 113 in 1860) and the miners (2,357). The businessmen faced the dilemma of decrying the drifting propensities of miners, hating the booms and busts associated with mining, yet remaining economically dependent on the mines. Since the miners tended to be foreigners, there were heavy overtones of 1850s nativism in the merchants' minds. Ethnic prejudice seriously divided the town's classes. The Cornish, with their skills in hard-rock mining, were contrasted with Irish, Chinese, and blacks in other types of labor. Miners held their own grievances, actually boycotting the water companies over rates in the year Josie was born and growing strong enough to strike against the companies eleven years later. By 1860 the wealthiest 1 percent of the county's residents owned 36 percent of its property, a figure approaching that of Boston and St. Louis at the time. The growth of the village caused the typical social, racial, and economic rifts that challenged the idea of an integrated community.

These basic conflicts impinged on the life of a boy chiefly through the institutions that reflected them. The church, for example, not only was segregated but was a prime tool of stability, heartily supported by the merchants. "Every good citizen," advised the newspaper, the voice of the merchants, "ought to attend some place of public worship, at least once on every Sabbath, if for no other purpose than to set a good example to the rising generation."

The Royces stood among the little band that did not need the advice. Wherever they wandered in this rough land, they found kindred spirits to unite with them in religious worship. Grass Valley provided the chance to go further into organized religion. When Josie was only three, his father and mother helped organize a congregation of the Disciples of Christ, or Christian Church. In the spring of 1859, the church trustees, including Royce, bought for $750 the property of the Sons of Temperance on the east side of Church Street. It included a two-story hall of lath and plaster styled "in the Grecian order." The Christian Church built its own meetinghouse, perhaps an addition to the Temperance Hall, at a cost of three thousand dollars. The church was one block above Mill Street and directly up from the Royce house. A shortcut path probably connected the two. Josiah, his friend Thomas Barr, a rancher Levi Sanford (who would later be his neighbor), and a physician, J. P. Blanks, were among the first trustees.

By then Grass Valley was growing beyond the "roughing it" phase of religion, too. In the earliest years missionaries from standard denominations like the Congregationalists came into the camps; they often wrote home of their discouragement. One minister felt like a beggar in a raucous society that cared little for his message. The Catholics did better, because of the large foreign groups. Worshiping in a small bare building since 1853, the Catholics raised St. Patrick's in the same year the Disciples built their church just down the block. The Episco-

Disciples' camp meeting. E. B. Ware's *History of the Disciples of Christ in California* (Healdsburg, Calif.: F. W. Cooke, 1916) included this rare photograph of an early camp meeting in the state. The Royce family embraced this denomination.

palians and the Methodists were in that block, too, and the Congregationalists met nearby.

The religious community rose like a small Gibraltar in the Grass Valley sea. The Disciples were particularly given to camp meetings, and on the Fourth of July 1856, Josie was undoubtedly carried to his first Sabbath school picnic. It was held in a grove about halfway between Grass Valley and Nevada City. A young worker, William Shepard, thought there were five hundred children there and twice that number of adults, a large turnout in a combined population of some seven thousand. His comments are a measure of the upbeat feelings about the event.

> A portion of the day spent by listening to the Honorables and Reverences with ever and anon a song by the Grass Valley juvenile quoir under charge of Mr. Holbrooke, teacher of vocal music. Nor was the day altogether occupied by speaking and singing for they had the long tables heaped with good things to eat and drink.

One part of the community of church and neighbors gathered at the Royce house for meetings and "sings." Sarah's melodeon provided the harmonic center. And these contacts ramified outward. Thomas Barr, for example, fellow member of the Christian Church, later became a partner with Royce in land ventures, and Thomas remained one of the family's oldest friends. When the Royces left Grass Valley, Barr followed them to San Francisco and became a founding member of the Christian Church there.

The larger community was no more than a collection of associations. Primitive government existed in Grass Valley since the miners elected an *alcalde* to punish thieves and settle claims. But not until 1855, the year of Josie's birth, did incorporated local government come to Grass Valley. The first board of trustees meeting on March 19, 1855, in the schoolhouse on Church Street, set its priorities by immediately proposing to lease a room in the brick building of the hardpressed Adams Express Company "for the use of the town as a watchhouse or jail." The subsequent four meetings were all involved with finding a detention cell, and thereafter that worry was interspersed with ordinances on shows, "the improper and indecent exposure of persons in the streets or other places," and the impounding of hogs running loose in the streets. A petition to remove a "house of ill-fame" was "lade" on the table. Pine-plank sidewalks were required at property owners' expense on both sides of Mill Street to a block or so beyond the Royce land. The fire danger was addressed in an ordinance to remove obstructions to the examination of stovepipes and chimneys. And all of these came before the appointment of a tax collector in October.

Aside from the provisions on fire and sidewalks, the new government of Grass Valley was most concerned with the imposition of gentility and morality. Rowdy shows, indecent exposure, and unbridled swine were not the images easily tolerated by Sabbath school picnickers like the Royces and Thomas Barr. But beyond the infant government's concern with gentility, the merchants looked on the essential restlessness in the mining part of their community like a seventh prudential sin. Sarah saw how these chronic prospectors "kept the whole community in a ferment."

We know now that mobility was virtually as high in eastern urban centers as it was in the West; nevertheless, the men of Grass Valley perceived too many of their fellow townsmen as transients. The Directory of 1865 used "drifter" as one category of occupation, and in one Grass Valley suburb (Allison Ranch) of 250, fully 103 were so identified. The merchants of Grass Valley pointed to roving miners as an unhappy base for a sound economy. Samuel Nichols wrote his wife from the area, "There are a great many stories, and very strange ones, too, got up for the purpose of an excitement in this new country." Even the mine owners called their workers "bereft of common prudence." It was an appropriate phrase for 1858, when Josie was three years old and miners everywhere streaked out of town to try their luck on the Fraser River in British Columbia. The editor of the *Telegraph* reported that four hundred men had left Grass Valley alone. The effect on the Royce fruit business must have been substantial.

Sarah saw herself, her family, and the church as a beseiged island in an ocean of immorality. In her memoirs she emphasized the generous, genteel, and gentle people, but it was her character to focus wishfully on them while her fundamentalist ethics searched for the contrast between good and evil. Hardly blind to the underside of her society, she, like William Shepard, knew how much card playing went on in Grass Valley, and she observed "habits gaining ground among the thoughtless and selfish which gave me uneasiness." She decried the custom of newly rich men lavishing presents on their lady acquaintances, even throwing jewelry and coins at the feet of young ladies on the stage, referring to the likes of her neighbor Lotta Crabtree. Divorce appalled her, and she tried not to blame California, but rather "shallow, weak natures in whom selfishness predominates" who were the kind to be tempted by the unfettered conditions of the frontier. She must have talked with her friends about the young men of the town who were

Sarah Eleanor Bayliss Royce. The youngest picture of Sarah, perhaps in San Francisco about 1867. Some of her uncomplicated faith and rigid devotion can be read into the pose, the braids, and the intense expression. (Courtesy of Nancy A. Hacker)

lured into a Boston Ravine saloon, where dancing girls who called themselves Hurdy Gurdies (after the saloon itself) had been plying their trade. In Nevada City the respectable volunteer fire brigade literally flushed out the Hurdies with fire hoses, but in Grass Valley the girls remained and worked not far from the Royces down Mill Street. In Sarah's eyes each of them was like the adulterous mother of three girls in her school: "How can she endure to think of the work *she* has wrought into the fabric of California social life?" Their morals were not far from the equation of money with success or happiness, and that was everywhere. She must have been appalled in the winter of 1858 when Michael Brennan killed his wife, three small children, and himself by prussic-acid poisoning because he feared that his bad luck with the Massachusetts Hill mine might impoverish his family.

The moral stance of the Royces underscored the fractures in the community. Basically it was a male population, over 90 percent of which was in its twenties and thirties and only 7 percent of which was married. According to the newspaper these men felt themselves to be only "lovers of fun and California liberty," and they frequently sneered at Christians. Of course, the strength of cultural norms rather than age was the chief factor. At least William Shepard held to the old values, on Sunday dutifully got himself "fixed up with standing collar," and joined the Royces and their friends in congregation. When he attended the Methodist church in December 1854, the sermon he heard compared California society with hell.

Inasmuch as Sarah's fundamentalism was tinged with a more outward-looking evangelicalism, her moral lighthouse was trained also on the surrounding sea of speculators, impractical enterprises, and shady credit. In what she called the lottery of mining, she observed reckless borrowing and extravagant expansion, but she also decried such practices in the cattle business and in land purchases. "These wild things" were everywhere. Issues of morality and social reform effectively bifurcated the society economically, institutionally, and ethnically. So it was in all small towns in America, but in the frontier setting the nature of the population intensified the contrast.

The last two years of the 1850s were hard times for Grass Valley. Nearly one-third of the miners left. One Cornishman wrote home, "California is now a poor country," and he simply could not support his family. The elder Royce was undoubtedly having his troubles, looking around for ways to better his lot. He and his friend Thomas Barr decided to buy more-productive land and sell their own produce. Thus about 1860, when Josie was five or six, the Royces moved from Neal Street to a frontier farm on the western edge of Grass Valley. Yet the move could not wipe from a boy's mind the color of a mining town that, like the taste of a ripe peach or a Mexican chili, he could not forget if he wanted to. It had been a rich experience to be remembered, and the new life would continue to be a rough environment to be transcended.

CHAPTER 3

Avon Farm

"Many souls in their young nudity are tumbled out among incongruities and left to 'find their feet' among them."
George Eliot, *Middlemarch*

ON December 22, 1857, Royce pooled his meager resources with those of his more affluent church friend Thomas Barr and, with their combined eight thousand dollars, bought the ranch of William Chollar, a mine owner who later gained some repute as "Uncle Billy" in the Washoe mines of Nevada. The land contained 150 acres, a considerable increase over the Royces' one acre in town. Its boundaries began at the site of the old Penobscott sawmill, and slab fences separated it from the ranches of Levi Sanford, a fellow trustee of the Christian Church; P. C. Huntley, a dairyman-neighbor from Neal Street; and the Gold Hill Ranch on the east. It was broken, wooded country with clearings in the trees for orchards and dairy cattle.

We do not know exactly when the Royces moved. The census of 1860 inexplicably fails to show them in either place. But on March 20, 1862, they sold their town lot to William Whiteside for two thousand dollars. By then they were certainly living on the farm to the west.

About this time Josiah left for a try at running a store in the Washoe mines, perhaps an idea he got from Chollar. Royce was absent for nearly three years, until January 1865. It was an unhappy time for him. A weak back often kept him down. The $2,500 he made in the store was eaten up by family expenses back home, creditors, and a robbery. He wrote his brother when he returned that he was "poorer than when I left," de-

Commencing at the north East corner of said ranch at a point about twenty rods northwardly from the Site formerly occupied by the Penobscot Saw Mill and say about fifty rods northeastwardly from the present Vallew House. Running thence westerly along the line of a slab fence eighty ing rods more or less till said fence in [intersects] land of W.O. Huntly thence Southerly along the line of a picket fence one hundred rods more or less till said fence which the land of Clem Sanford and Company thence Easterly along the line of a slab fence ninety rods more or less till said fence strikes the Ogee Hill ranch fence Northerly along the line of a slab fence one hundred and fifty rods more or less to the place of beginning: being the Eastern boundary line of said ranch; and containing one hundred and fifty acres of land be the same more or less.

Deed to Avon Farm. The descriptive portion of the deed of William Chollar to Josiah Royce, Sr., and Thomas Barr, December 22, 1857. Note the farmhouse, the Penobscot sawmill, the neighboring ranches, the slab and the picket fences. (Courtesy of Nevada County Recorder's Office) pressed, and fearing that he would be forced to go on public works.

The move was thus related to Josiah's financial bad luck and his consequent restlessness, but the times provided other possible reasons. Hard conditions for the merchants beginning in 1855 were seriously exacerbated by the national depression following 1857. A further blow came in 1858, with the population outflow to the Fraser River. Royce may have believed that producing more of his own fruit and dairy products on a larger farm would give him an economic advantage. The same idea led him to settle outside Folsom in 1853. From Sarah's standpoint, the change removed her family from immediate contact with the town's immoral elements.

The purchase included an orchard and a barn; in 1865 Barr, who appeared the responsible owner, was taxed on an additional two horses and a wagon. The crowning improvement, however, was the two-story framed farmhouse, painted white with a stone-lined cellar and a well near the kitchen door. On three sides of the house ran a porch from which the children remembered watching the sunsets, looking out over the orchard, a broad green meadow, and a "wilderness of rocks and bushes" below. Barr lived in one room and the cellar. The rest was for the Royces.

The land was as good as the area offered. It was not prime valley farmland, and Easterners such as William Shepard, with his Ohio farm in mind, could easily deride it. He complained that within six miles of Grass Valley there were only half a dozen acres of good land sufficiently watered by springs: "By far the greatest portion of the land in this area would not bear white beans without well manuring and carefully irrigating, and a sparce crop at that." Nevertheless, plenty of farms were going in, especially orchards, and the region was coming to be known as the Bartlett Pear Belt. The Royces did have available irrigation water from Squirrel Creek, since the springs that formed its headwaters rose only a stone's throw from their door.

They called it Avon Farm, a wishful recall of Sarah's birthplace on the gently flowing English Avon. The orderliness of English hedgerows bore precious little comparison with these wild hills, but Sarah was determined to project, even through nomenclature, the values of her simple rural past now transplanted. For her the new land presented an opportunity to expand the culture of the old. The boy must have heard from his mother something of the meaning of Avon.

On this farm Josie spent crucially formative years till he was eleven. Here crystallized the memories that would persist into later life. Here developed his mind's first complex memory strategies, the first uses of concepts and prototypes. Here attention began to focus on more than the immediate and the most prominent. Here the handling of symbols emerged through his reading. And these crucial changes came to him in an Acadian setting surrounded by a society of recent Argonauts.

The town of Grass Valley was one and a half miles away, close enough for constant contact, far enough to intensify observations of its growth. And its growth was dramatic. In the ten years the Royces lived in Grass Valley, the population of the township increased from around fifteen hundred to over five thousand. When Sarah now walked her boy down Mill and Main streets, the plank sidewalks were more frequent, but not yet complete. They would still pass Denman's carriage shop and the smithy, but three other livery stables competed nearby. There was now a Photograph and Ambrotype Gallery, which specialized in pictures of deceased persons. Sarah could choose from five grocery stores and six dry-goods stores. There were at least five saloons and two liquor stores for her to hurry by. Main Street alone counted five hotels.

The directory of 1865 boasted seven churches and a synagogue, nine schools, eight fraternal orders, two daily newspapers, and two banks, one of which belonged to Alonzo Delano, the humorist nicknamed Old Block, who came to Grass Valley to work for Wells Fargo. The telegraph line connected with Grass Valley by 1861, and its agent, William Spencer, took messages in his Book and News Depot on Main

Street. That, combined with the Pony Express arrivals in Sacramento, caused the *National* to ask, "What is to be the limit of human progress in the aniation [i.e., annihilation] of time and space!" The first gas illumination (manufactured from pitch pine and stone coal) came to town in 1862. And since Josie's father was a merchant, though a small one, the family would be counted in the restricted circle of businessmen, numbering only 4 percent of the population in 1860; three-quarters of the people, the miners, remained socially far below them.

In the boy's years there, Grass Valley's growth from a hustling village to a stable community was, on the one hand, a typical American frontier story. The middle-class merchants withdrew to their own neighborhoods, attended their own churches, and looked askance at the vices of the foreigners in other districts. Race and class lines solidified.

On the other hand, Grass Valley's rapid growth and its skewed, heavily male population suggested its unusual qualities. There were still three to four men for every woman, though that was a better balance than the ten to one when Josie was born. By 1865 only about 20 percent of the men were married, still very low but considerably higher than the 5 percent in 1855. The boy's contacts outside the family were largely adult because the town numbered relatively few children.

The mentality of Grass Valley lingered with its frontier past. Indians in 1860 occasionally walked the streets, visiting from a nearby reservation, and the townsfolk easily remembered the spring of 1850, when one hundred miners in a couple of days "killed and run off all the Indians." Several residents were numbered proudly "among the Indian exterminators." Likewise, there were still episodes of violence—"Judge Lynch" administering thirty-six lashes, "painfully frequent" mining accidents, and land disputes (four men were killed in a land tussle three years after Josie was born). These may have been abnormal events, but they were agonizingly evident.

Major fires continued to gut the downtown area: a big one in 1860 and two more in 1862. Independent fire companies came and went; in 1863 the Tiger Hook, Ladder, and Bucket

Company had grasped for permanence by appointing as honorary member the local editor, John Rollin Ridge, author of the first literary legend of Joaquin Murieta. Fire, as the newspaper said, was "California's most dreaded domestic enemy."

There remained other visibly rough edges. Pigs still ran the streets; the city council in 1861 increased fines for the offending owners to twenty dollars. At the same time, it became unlawful to ride any animal through town "in a furious manner." Roaming cows were being impounded, and irate owners were cautioned by the newspaper to remember that "this transition state of society between town and city life, is always a little awkward and inconvenient, at first."

Grass Valley was by now a mining labor town, but nearly half of those laborers were from Great Britain and Ireland. The Irish had two saloons, McSorley's and McGuire's, and tended to live apart. The labor force included a high percentage of Cornishmen, those shrewd, skillful, independent "Cousin Jacks." The Chinese, like the Irish, were segregated. The boy must have walked often by the small Grass Valley Chinatown, where he could see temples, a theater, and dragon-decorated restaurants. The inhabitants were almost wholly young males, excluded from work in the quartz mines, and the few women were assumed to be prostitutes. The only time it was popular to visit Chinatown was during the New Year's celebration, for generally the Chinese were seen as "a queer people." The newspaper in 1861 snidely remarked that one Chinaman had just put up his winter provisions, "a hind quarter of a horse and two barrels of bull-dogs." They were constantly blamed for thefts, even for counterfeiting silver dollars.

Not surprisingly, the town was wanting in cultural attributes. Gibbs Paint Store advertised "the finest engravings" in its gallery, and the Sylvania Debating Society held meetings in connection with the Templars, but the Royces probably avoided these attractions, just as they did entertainments such as the panoramas of exotic lands, the vaudeville acts of Yankee Locke, or the balls in Hamilton Hall on New Year's Eve and

Washington's Birthday. These were community attractions before Grass Valley families transferred such events into their
own houses, but religious proscriptions against dancing and
theatricals undoubtedly kept the Royces away. Josiah later
contended that his childhood had been deficient in exposure
to the beautiful, and that must have included public entertain-
ment as well.

It is hard to believe that the boy did not work around Avon
Farm. Pears ripened and had to be picked in the late summer;
apples, in the fall. There were probably Concord grape vines,
and maybe strawberries, acres of which were set out around
Grass Valley in 1856. Horses needed tending, cows milking,
and butter churning. In Grass Valley today there is a tradition
that young Royce delivered milk in town, and a bright ten- or
eleven-year-old lad could certainly have done the job. If, however, the boy was a part of the farm's labor, it is curious that
there is no extant mention of such in his later life. Unlike John
Muir, who wrote as if his farm work, as much as he hated it,
led directly into his mature naturalism, Royce either did not
have or suppressed these agrarian connections.

It is more likely that the boy worked little, if at all, in the
orchards and pastures. His sister Ruth described her brother
as without "mechanical tastes and [with] little bodily agility."
Stephen Royce once told an interviewer that his father had
suffered as a boy from a siege of rheumatic fever, a not un-
common disease at the time. A streptococcus throat was followed by swollen joints, and the ailment frequently damaged
the valves of the heart. The cardiac threat often led to prescrip-
tions of reduced physical labor. Then, too, Josie was an asth-
matic, a condition he inherited from his mother and shared
with his sisters. It was a lifetime affliction. The asthma with
the possible additional worries from rheumatic fever abun-
dantly explain his mother's concern for her boy and her pro-
tective stance, leading to her emphasis on intellectual pursuits
for him.

Nature, however, remained a sustaining element in Royce's
thinking and writing. The woods were of ponderosa and sugar

pine, black oak, fir, and cedar. They were a rich playground. On their Indian trails, he could gather arrowheads and mortars. He could peer at a Nisenan tribal burial ground only half a mile to the south. If adventurous, he could explore ruins. The Penobscott sawmill on the edge of their land was now a jumble of rusting iron and skewed boards, with mounds of moist, molding sawdust. Abandoned mines were scattered over the hills—coyote diggings, they called them in town, little more than mounds of earth pushed up in hope, then deserted.

He could fish for trout in Squirrel Creek, especially when it ran full in the spring. Wild blackberries were ripe in the summer. Deer and red fox, coyotes and brown bears, quail and pigeons, robins, chickadees, and blackbirds lived thereabouts. He later wrote of a little boy who saw a snake "down where the moss grew" and looked for it every day wanting to take it to bed with him at night. What he remembered most about the woods were the points at which the trees would stop and the rocky slopes below would roll away toward Penn Valley, where the Indians lived, and beyond to the wide Sacramento Valley. He described it in one of his writings:

> the whole immense river valley itself seemed at the end of our walk to flash of a sudden into existence before our eyes, with all its wealth of shining and winding streams, with the "Three Buttes" near Marysville, springing up like young giants from the midst of the plain, and with the beautiful, long, and endlessly varied blue line of the Coast Range bounding the noble scene on the west.

The boy became closely bonded with nature. Throughout his life it remained a sustenance for him. He said once that in these years he hoped to be a hunter or a trapper—lonely ambitions, but close to the woods and streams. Later, whenever his physical or mental frame gave out, he found immersion in nature to be his best renewal, often freighting on a sea voyage to the Caribbean. He wrote rhetorically of messages sent to his wife by the sea birds. Even his philosophical prose was laced with natural images.

Yet Josie was not an outdoor boy—certainly not the kind of outdoorsperson who thinks of nature as something to be conquered or mastered. His sisters remembered him, not outdoors, but with a book, and more likely a book about history than about birds or animals. Nature for the boy was a setting for the imagination, a chance to think and to dream. When he was a man of sixty, he remembered from these days the vestiges of diggings, among which he noted "that many pine logs were rotten, and that a miner's grave was to be found in a lonely place not far from my own house." With their solitary, imaginative tone, the words say much about the boy but also ring true to the place and time. Not long afterward, the Grass Valley city council passed an ordinance against indiscriminate burials throughout the local woods, and the year the Royces left Avon Farm, William C. Pope, a local cabinetmaker and undertaker, opened a cemetery less than half a mile east of the Royce house. The memory of a lonely grave echoed Grass Valley days when there was no city council to regulate burial places.

Like many another six- and seven year-old, the boy began seriously to contemplate death. He had experienced no bereavement in his immediate family, and in that respect he had an unusual frontier childhood. Family tales, however, must have recalled the death of his newborn brother John Samuel, but that was before Josie was born. It was rather, he later felt, that lonely grave near his house that inspired his thoughts on death. In a high school composition he remembered that burial place. In a "dusty, dry, flowerless, and unfertile" spot "a rough-hewn shingle proclaimed the existence of a grave, where lonely and forsaken some one once loved, once full of hope, rested again with the love and hope so long forgotten."

Nature was a source for Josie's imagination, and so, too, was his voracious reading. The Bible was always available, as was John Bunyan's *Pilgrim's Progress*, and the boy pored over these until they became a part of him. In fact, the first story he deciphered on his own was the Apocalypse, "from a large print New Testament, which I found on the table in our living

room." Bear in mind that this is a boy under ten who is
reading:

> And I turned to see the voice that spake with me. And being
> turned, I saw seven golden candlesticks; and in the midst of
> the seven candlesticks one like unto the Son of man, clothed
> with a garment down to the foot, and girt about the paps with
> a golden girdle. . . . And he had in his right hand seven stars;
> and out of his mouth went a sharp two-edged sword; and his
> countenance was as the sun shineth in his strength.

He admitted later that "the Apocalypse did not tend to teach
me early to acquire very clear ideas."

Sometime in these years Royce set out on a religious path
different from the fundamentalist attachments of his mother
and father. "The observance of Sunday," he said, "aroused
from an early time a certain more or less passive resistance,
which was stubborn, although seldom, I think, openly re-
bellious." His rising indifference to church and camp meetings, to the sermons and hymn singing must have pained
his mother, but in these days Royce was seeding his lifetime's apathy toward organized religion. "I was a born non-
conformist," he said, though he never rejected religion as such,
only its overt forms, and he could not unlearn his close attachment to the Bible. In one of his later writings, Royce described an "odd and reserved" man who found his religious
satisfaction "in being the sole member of a religious sect. You
need not propagate the faith, you are relieved from all the rivalry of fellow-worshipers, you enjoy alone the sacred fountains." In his Avon Farm boyhood Josie began to enjoy the
sacred fountains on his own.

Around the time they moved to Avon Farm, desperate for
money in her husband's long Nevada absence, Sarah took a
teaching job in the public school. The Grass Valley directory
of 1865 lists her as the school's only primary-grade teacher,
with ninety-six pupils. They met in the high school building
on School Street, one block above the Christian Church. Sarah
and at times the older children walked the mile to school each

day, so Josie and his sisters remained his mother's pupils whether at school or at home.

We do not know precisely at what times the older children attended the public school and when they studied at home. But even when in school the children must have returned to the farm before the mother. Mary Eleanor, the oldest, remembered the routine of those years. Just before their mother was expected home from school, the children were to put the house in good order and set the table in the high-ceilinged sitting room with its green-figured wall paper.

> Supper, or dinner as the city people call it, was generally a very cheerful meal for us; for as Mother had been away all day, we children had all the day's employment and pleasures to relate to her; and she, in return, often had ammusing [sic] or interesting anneddotes [sic] to relate about her scholars. After supper was disposed of, the table was drawn out, the lamp placed upon it, and we all gathered around it to spend our evening.

In these lamplit nights, talking, reading stories from the Bible, or quietly working to the tick of the old clock on the bookcase, Sarah and her children detached themselves from the world. They thought of their father, gone for three of these years, but it was only to wish him back. It was Sarah around whom this world revolved.

As long as they were in the Grass Valley area, Josie's learning was supervised by his mother and his sisters. Mary Eleanor taught him to read. Their home library was expanding. As early as 1854 Sarah claimed in her school advertisements that she would be teaching from books such as *Watts on the Mind*, a History of England, Mrs. Lincoln's *Larger Botany*, John Comstock's *System of Natural Philosophy*, *Geography of the Heavens*, Samuel Phillips Newman's *Practical System of Rhetoric*, and John Abercrombie's *Inquiries Concerning the Intellectual Powers*. Books like these must have been in her personal library. Mary Eleanor brought home books from school, such as G. P.

Quackenbos's *A Natural Philosophy: Embracing the Most Recent Discoveries in the Various Branches of Physics*. (In her copy, someone wrote "Jo Royce.") Books could be bought in town. J. P. Blanks sold them in his drug store on Mill Street. William K. Spencer, the telegraph agent, carried books along with newspapers and musical instruments on Main Street. The Grass Valley newspaper in 1861 even listed new arrivals at H. H. Bancroft's San Francisco shop: Headley's *Life of Scott*, Buckle's *History of Civilization in England*, and Charles Lever's *Day's Ride*. If and when they had the money, sources of building a library were not far off for the Royces.

For Christmas of 1865, when Josie was ten, his mother gave him a copy of Phineas Camp Headley's *The Miner Boy and His Monitor; or, the Career and Achievements of John Ericsson, the Engineer*. The clergyman-author hoped that he might encourage "young hearts in their life work," and it is possible that Royce here changed his hopes from hunter-trapper to engineer. Ericsson certainly provided a heroic model—an intellectual boy in a secluded Swedish mining town training himself with book and pencil, going on to revolutionize the ships of the world. With God as his witness, "work, work is the history of John." If Royce was inspired by Ericsson's life, the stimulation came sometimes in the woods, for among the pages of Josie's book, still extant, are pressed columbine blossoms.

Sometimes his reading, the woods, and the outcropping hills with their long views came vividly together. When he was nine or ten, he read astronomy, probably books used in his mother's instruction on the geography of the heavens. Then in his own experience at night, contemplating the numbers and distances of the stars,

> I came to seem so far from home; and the contemplation of the mere magnitude of Being gave me a choking in the throat, and a lonely kind of fear,—a fear which seemed all the more hopeless because nothing that I could conceivably do, or could pray God to do, or could hope for, could be expected to alter in the least the essential situation, or make this cold world

of the beautiful stars and the terrible distances comfortably smaller.

His mother must have assigned him to write a good deal. One such effort written when he was eight or nine still exists: "Pussy Blackie's Travels." The typescript copy retains spelling and sentence errors, which make its thirty-one pages the more remarkable, because believable.

Pussy Blackie's journey throws light on life at Avon Farm. The story begins in a farmhouse on the side of a hill about a mile from town, not far from a cabin of bachelors. Blackie belonged to the three sisters and younger boy of Mrs. Royce, a public school teacher about forty-five years of age (Sarah would have been forty-five in 1865). The cat was left alone during the day. Feeling forsaken, he ran away and was taken into a mansion by Lucy Andrews, a rich girl with an Irish maid. Unliked by the maid, the cat moved on across the Sierras to Washoe, where he was fed by the "husband and father" of the Royces, who ran a grocery store there. Continuing his journey, Blackie was bitten by a mad dog in Salt Lake City, made the sport of a mean boy, and saved by another dog from the horrors of a burning hotel. The young author called the latter detail "a fact"; perhaps a dog had rescued a cat in some Grass Valley fire. Somewhere near St. Louis, an eagle seized Blackie and bore him aloft, but the cat scratched the eagle's throat until "the blood came in great amounts," another fact, the author claimed. Aboard a railroad car, Blackie was carried to Cincinnati, identified as the city of "all pork! pork! pork!" Here he dreamed of a child being refused help by men who called the urchin a "beggar's brat." The cat took refuge in the house of a rich pork merchant where a young lady, Lucretia, read Sir Walter Scott's "Lady of the Lake" and debated with her brother over passages such as "FitzJames in the Pass of the Trossacks." He quoted a verse:

> Wild as the scream of the curlew,
> From crag to crag the signal flew.
> Instant, through copse and heath, arose
> Bonnets and spears and bended bows.

Here Blackie found a cat companion with whom he exchanged stories about the values of honesty and the evils of pride and ambition. The two traveled by steamboat up the Ohio to Pittsburgh, where they were trapped in a large hole, or mine. Expecting to die, the friend forgave Blackie for all his untruthfulness. But through cracks and tunnels and inclines and cave-ins, the two survived. Intending now to go home, they crept into railroad cars that carried them instead to Richmond. The city was filled with soldiers dressed in blue.—"I wonder what soldiers ar[e] good for in the world," said Blackie. And there, musing about guns and war, the story ended.

This childhood fantasy tells us much about what the young Royce experienced in his Avon Farm life: the family, literary discussion, the father away in Washoe, the bachelor miners, the fires, the mines, perhaps even the mean boys. Josie obviously had studied geography and knew the world east of the Sierras, at least Salt Lake City, St. Louis, the Mississippi, the Ohio, Cincinnati, Pittsburgh, and Richmond. And there were moral questions of honesty, shame, killing, and war, issues that the boy-grown-man, America's great philosopher, wrestled with all his life. Blackie, too, may be seen as the alter ego of the boy. In raising social implications, portraying the contrast between rich and poor, even the treatment of a beggar's brat, he moved into a more evangelical, less fundamentalist worldview. With hazard after hazard, Blackie learns to live by his intelligence. The cat and the boy are each lonely creatures who will break out of their isolated existence through applications of wit and learning. Prophetically their trek is eastward.

In these years, Josie became aware of the national scene that was crashing apart into civil war, "the dark shadow of great sorrow which overspreads our late happy land," as the newspaper put it. When in town, he could hardly have missed the frequent debates, the columns in the newspapers, the calls for volunteers, the speakers on the stump before the Exchange

Hotel (in August 1861 the town was averaging six to eight political speakers a week, including Leland Stanford and Charles Crocker). Grass Valley was a Democratic stronghold, partly because of its foreigners, and when the war broke out, the town was thought to harbor copperheads. One editor called it "the Charleston of California." In 1861 an anti-Lincoln, anti-equality speaker was quoted at length in the newspaper: "four millions of semi-savages. Are we to turn them loose upon society?" Royce remembered as a boy hearing much about the conflict, reflected in his inclusion of Richmond in Pussy Blackie's itinerary.

Josie was nine when Lincoln was assassinated. In his later fiction one of his characters, desolate at Lincoln's death, "felt as if his own father was gone." "Thenceforth," Royce later wrote, "I had a country as well as a religious interest." He implied here that his earliest years revolved around religion. True, his community began with his mother's faith, but broader national and political ideas now impinged. Along with their expansion, he was granted his own release from the strictures of a remote mining town. In the overall life of Josiah Royce, it was important that he leave Grass Valley for the wider world.

The Royces abandoned their rights to Avon Farm on January 13, 1862, about the time Josiah left for Washoe. On November 7 that year they sold their interest in the property to Thomas Barr. As a friend, Barr let Sarah and the children stay on the farm after the sale, and the family did not leave Grass Valley for some years. Royce may have needed the money for the venture in the Comstock. Apparently he lost most of it there. A cryptic entry in the county assessor's books for 1865, the year he returned from the debacle in Nevada, shows "Cleveland and Royce" paying $34.30 tax on eight horses, one wagon, and a coach, valued at $1,400. It would seem that the father was involved in something like a livery stable, undoubtedly another abortive enterprise.

The Royces left Avon Farm for San Francisco in 1866. We can only conjecture why. Though times were generally bad for mining in the late 1860s, in the Grass Valley area following 1865 there was new prosperity due to an expansion of local quartz mining. It is possible that this expansion in itself worried Sarah, as more and more of the rougher mining element moved into the rural areas surrounding them. By the 1860s the hills for miles around Grass Valley were becoming denuded, and there was concern about deforestation. More important, probably, was Sarah's perception that her only son was ready for educational advantages that neither she nor Grass Valley could provide.

Young Josie was by now clearly what the modern world would call gifted. Whether Sarah, in teaching him herself and at this crucial juncture moving the family to the city, was acting on that assumption, we will never know. More interesting is the question of how an exceptional child reacts to frontier conditions. Isabella Bird found on the American frontier "the extinction of childhood" with a ten-year-old treated like an adult and children shrewd and old for their age. Would the bright pioneer child enter adulthood still more rapidly? Psychologists tell us that exceptional children show abnormal ability to "organize" their own environments, to select from their surroundings what will be most important to their future achievements. Royce seemed to be doing something like this. His immersion in the world of Avon Farm, rather than narrowing his horizons, became an expansion of his imagination readying him, among other things, for the message of the romantic poets. An internal drive led him to take advantage of his years of freedom from the public school to push into poetry and history and mathematics.

Royce's giftedness led to creativity and achievement, first, because of his family situation. His father's frequent absence at least avoided the interference of one parent, and it allowed his mother to control his intellectual and moral development. She set the intellectual tone of the household; her gifts for language stimulated similar gifts in the child; her warmth and affection made effective discipline possible (requiring his si-

lence); her concerns for his health allowed him relative re-
prieve from the chores of the farm.

Some studies show the most creative individuals coming
from families in which there is some tension, and it is possible
that Sarah and the elder Royce did feel some such discord,
remembering Sarah's frustrations with the frequent moves and
her consequent inability to settle down into a quiet Christian
community. On top of the tension, though, there must be a
family commitment to achievement, and certainly Sarah was a
woman who lived for the creation of a moral society. Other
studies have shown that eminent men outside of the sciences
have tended to be mother oriented in childhood (examples
being Freud, Gandhi, and Goethe, among many others).
From this relationship, "the child derives his feelings of being
'special'—of being preferred, favored, and selected for great
things." Furthermore, the exceptional child shows the capacity
to work alone, including the ability to handle physical isolation, as on a lonely farm outside a mining town. Eminent
minds, on the other hand, tend to be spurred by one or two
nonparental individuals; Royce's sisters Ruth and Mary
Eleanor seemed to have served that function.

These family relations along with his environment sharpened his innate curiosity. That same environment seems also
to have led him to a reasonable balance between a need for
independence based on lonely action and a need for achievement based on the opinions of others. His own philosophy
would later claim that the social dimension, the comparison
with others, was the essential ingredient in the freeing of the
individual, and thinking back on his experiences at Avon
Farm, Royce, the mature philosopher, could see it happening
in his own life.

Psychology aside, common sense alone tells us that earliest
memories are uneven, unpredictable, "gapped and rutted." In
Ivan Doig's words, "Childhood is a most queer flame-lit and
shadow-chilled time." In the lamplight of the parlor table
while his mother read aloud from the Bible, in the shadowed

woods where blackberry thickets concealed snakes and un-known miner's graves, on the planked sidewalks of a town that searched for identity, a red-haired, intellectually gifted boy, who would later write that he "neither can nor would outgrow his healthy local traits," was taking the steps that would some-day make him a distinguished philosopher.

CHAPTER 4

San Francisco

To know intense joy without a strong bodily frame, one must have an enthusiastic soul.

Eliot, *Middlemarch*

We know what a masquerade all development is, and what effective shapes may be disguised in helpless embryos. In fact, the world is full of hopeful analogies and handsome dubious eggs called possibilities.

Eliot, *Middlemarch*

IN 1866 the Royces returned to San Francisco. Sixteen years earlier Sarah and Josiah, their baby Mary Eleanor, and the residents of the house of "tenements" celebrated the admission of California into the Union. Then a raucous city of some 15,000, San Francisco now exceeded 100,000, having doubled in the years of the Civil War alone. Striking growth only emphasized its restive and unsettled qualities; the Royces were hardly incongruous in a time and place that motivated three out of four workers to leave within eight years of their arrival.

The same restlessness, combined as it was with sudden wealth for a few, had at least been coincidental with literature. Mark Twain barely preceded the Royces' return to San Francisco and published his first successful story, "The Celebrated Jumping Frog of Calaveras County," that very year. But like Lola Montez abandoning Grass Valley, Twain departed on a European voyage just after the Royces arrived. He left behind a literary friend, Bret Harte, who a few months later became the editor of a new journal, the *Overland Monthly*. Royce as a young man would write for that magazine, but he never liked its first editor's romantic stories of the California mines. The lives of Harte and Royce, physically contingent for a time, were worlds apart. Harte not only was a romantic writer, but he himself played a role that suggested the gaiety and cosmopolitanism of San Francisco, dressing foppishly and hobnobbing with literary circles that included Jessie Benton Frémont. It was no more the world of Sarah and Josiah Royce than were either the Hurdy Gurdy girls or the Cornish miners of Grass Valley. Yet this City of Destruction was the San Francisco that Josie observed as he began to tramp each morning to his new grammar school.

The Royces lived on Folsom between Sixth and Seventh streets, a crowded, working-class neighborhood with industrial buildings—a brewery, a sugar refinery, a smithy—scattered among the houses. The brightest relief in their block was a small park on the south side of the street, a poor substitute for the woods of Avon farm. As in Grass Valley, single men were the majority in the neighborhood. The Royce house was large enough to be used for a store in the front, remembered by one visitor as "a little fruit store in a little house on the corner of the street." There Sarah presided, tending and selling the produce. Meanwhile Josiah drove a wagon through the streets hawking pears and apples. The same visitor to the fruit store described Josie's father at the time as "an odd-looking man" who was so fond of discussion that he would easily forget about selling his fruit. The neighbor boys called him crazy, "a little cracked in the head."

Josie entered the Lincoln Grammar School, an impressive four-story cruciform stone structure at the corner of Market and Fifth streets. Proudly dedicated only two years previous, the building accommodated nine hundred boys in classrooms of fifty. Josie could walk to school, no more than six blocks from the house on Folsom, but it must have been with some anxiety that a boy from Avon Farm faced such an edifice, climbing each morning the long front steps beside the imposing statue of Abraham Lincoln, a sobering memorial to the man so recently assassinated.

The first principal, Ira G. Hoitt, was a Knights Templar and

Lincoln Grammar School. The newly constructed school at Market and Fifth streets, San Francisco. Note the statue of the recently assassinated president. (Courtesy of the Huntington Library)

a scholarly man. With or without realizing it, the boy was indebted to him for establishing in the new school a small library that "afforded the pupils good reading at a time when public libraries were unknown."

That library may have been Josie's refuge, for he needed some respite from a boy's world he had till then never known. One of his classmates, Samuel P. Hall, later remembered Royce as "a poor little boy, wearing very seedy clothes." More important, "he did not have it in him to mix with other boys. He did not know how. The result was that the boys made fun of him and teased him in many ways." Hall explained Royce's treatment by his physical appearance, not just the carrot-red hair, but "an unusually small body and a very large head." Royce himself may have come closer when he explained the hazing by his own tendency "to preach down to what I supposed to be the level of these other boys." In any case, Hall's account fits with Royce's own memory of that school.

> My comrades very generally found me disagreeably striking in my appearance, by reason of the fact that I was redheaded, freckled, countrified, quaint, and unable to play boys' games. The boys in question gave me my first introduction to the "majesty of the community." The introduction was impressively disciplinary and persistent. On the whole it seemed to me "not joyous but grievous." In the end it probably proved to be for my good.

The "majesty of the community" played its part in defining the boy's own identity. If, as Royce would later claim, the individual slowly comes to know himself through comparison and imitation of others, then surely when others reject, it becomes important to identify oneself outside their circles. He would play no part in schoolyard games any more than he would cavort in the saloons with Lotta Crabtree or in the dandy haunts of Bret Harte. Yet such opposites had their uses, their essential functions for personal growth. For Royce, exclusion would become the extreme form of difference, with which we measure ourselves, against which we fight in the inevitable, eternal struggle. He may have outgrown his Grass Valley desire to be a hunter or a trapper, but the San Francisco schoolyard was keeping him equally lonely. Pussy Blackie was pursuing his singular path.

Royce claimed that there were exceptions to the bullies among his classmates, some even becoming lifelong friends. One special case was Sam Hall, who, feeling kindly toward Josie and once noticing his absence from school, looked him up at home. He found him in the back of the Folsom Street house in a woodshed, lying in some straw on the bare ground with an old quilt for bedding. The boy suffered from typhoid fever and probably lay in the shed as a quarantine from his three sisters in the house.

If friends like Sam Hall were few, many students remembered him, for whatever reasons. The school held a reunion in 1912, for which it sent out autobiographical questionnaires.

Though Royce, then a busy, nationally recognized philosopher, failed to return his own form, many did, and when asked to list the fellow students still remembered, they frequently named him; occasionally a student, like one Joseph Rothschild, recalled only Royce. Since by the time of the questionnaire Royce was well known, his renown may have influenced the results, but these former pupils were from all walks of life, and it is doubtful that many of them were touched by a philosopher's fame.

Through a happy chance, while Josie was there, the grammar school class of a young girl by the name of Fannie Cheney was invited to visit his school, and her composition book opens a door to us on Royce's education. The girls were to hear the debate between the Washington and Franklin clubs, and Fannie described the eagerly awaited event.

> A little after one o'clock the boys marched into the hall with military precision, to the music of the piano, and the beating of a drum. . . . The exercises were opened by the chanting of the "Lord's Prayer." Then we were welcomed by a boy from each of the first grades. After this we were asked to sing; this request we complied with by singing "May Flowers."

Fannie was not much interested in the subject of the debate: "Was the Mexican War justified or not?" She did not "see any use in boys meddling with such topics as these," but we can be relatively sure that one of the boys, Josie Royce, who may conceivably have been one of the debaters, was interested. Not only was Josiah drawn to history in his earliest Grass Valley reading, but he certainly heard from his mother the importance of the Mexican War in winning California, the dream of their family hegira. Interestingly enough, the subject would dominate many years of Royce's life, and this day in 1869 may have been one of the seeds in its flowering.

The visitation event, however, was not over. Fannie went on: "One of the lady teachers then led the boys through their calisthenics, after which each of the classes was represented in declamations, songs, etc." After the singing of "America," a half hour of social dancing followed. The principal then said,

"The next dance would be performed by the boys alone, and much to their discomfort marched them down stairs. So, ended our pleasant afternoon."

As Fannie's composition indicated, there was a good deal of public recitation in the curriculum. On one such occasion, a Saturday night, December 19, 1868, thirty-six students of the school presented songs, piano and violin pieces, skits, and declamations. David Belasco, the future theater writer and producer, was one of them, but Josiah Royce was not. The happenstance of David Belasco and Josiah Royce as products and schoolmates of gold-rush San Francisco caused John Clendenning to ponder the way each used the common experience. Belasco, the extrovert, dramatized and romanticized the frontier as in his *Girl of the Golden West* (the exuberant play that became Puccini's libretto), while Royce turned inward, criticized the frontier experience, and sought its deeper meanings.

The nature of Josie's school may also be suggested by an incident that occurred in 1870, just after Royce left Lincoln for high school. One John Goldsmith, aged fourteen, who had been four years at Lincoln School, was detained after hours "for failing to recite a lesson in Analysis satisfactorily, which lesson had been given them the day previous to be learned, over night, at home." At about four o'clock the teacher heard the class again and dismissed thirty who had mastered it. The remainder, including John Goldsmith, were allowed twenty minutes more to study the lesson. By now Goldsmith was "giving little or no attention to his book." The teacher prepared to rap him on the hands, but he resisted. A submaster was called in, but the boy refused to take his punishment, thrusting his hands "deep into the pockets of his pantaloons." He was then whipped from twenty to thirty times until he held out his hand. The subsequent report on the incident justified the punishment "for persistent disobedience and open defiance to the authority of the teacher."

The school was disciplined, drilled, and regimented, far from the self-modulated pace of Grass Valley. The Lincoln School boys did not walk, they marched from place to place.

Authority was evident and unquestioned. What Royce ironically called the "majesty of the community" was not only the boys and their treatment of him but might also have included the authority that controlled the school and ultimately the mob instinct. For the future philosopher such discipline was not bad, for it was authority exerted in a good cause, the cause of learning and social order. And the situation probably gladdened the puritanical propensities in his mother's mind, hopefully steeling a child against the delights of Bypath Meadow.

All the while, however, Sarah maintained her grip. On January 1, 1869, his last year in grammar school, she gave him a Bible inscribed with a long poem that ended:

> A mother's blessing on her son
> Goes with this holy thing.
> The love that would retain the one,
> Must to the other cling.
> Remember! 'tis no idle toy,
> A Mother's gift! Remember, boy!

In the book lay a petit point marker embroidered "For My Darling."

If young Royce was the butt of the boys' jokes and an also-ran in the declamation contests, he was nevertheless advancing intellectually. His first published work evidenced such progress. It appeared in a four-page newspaper, the *Lincoln Observer*, "published by the pupils of Lincoln School" in June 1869, his last month there. The essay, probably a class exercise, asked, "Is the Assassination of Tyrants Ever Justifiable?" The boy of thirteen, who entered his school each day in the shadow of a martyred president and later said that his first political instincts had been awakened by the assassination of Lincoln, answered with a qualified no. "In the first place it [assassination] is in opposition to the general rules of order and decency. . . . Such a course is the same as lynch law, which every one believes to be wrong." The young Royce did allow that a majority could justify acts of violence in the service of revolution, but "the assassination of a king or ruler by a conspiracy or by a single person, except by Divine command, has never done anything but harm, and from its very nature can do nothing else." In the proviso "except by Divine command," the voice of the Old Testament, the voice of Sarah Royce, still spoke loud and clear to the boy.

The essay was his swan song at Lincoln. It was the spring that the first trains over the transcontinental railroad steamed into Oakland. While California joined the great community of America, Royce widened his circle by entering San Francisco Boys' High School. On Powell between Clay and Sacramento, the school was an additional nine or ten blocks from Folsom Street, but trolleys ran on both Market and Powell. The building, compared to his grammar school, was a monstrosity. Cramped between other structures, "half brick, half wood, ungainly, inconvenient and no particular credit to the site it occupied," it was a refurbished church, but it looked more like a remodeled factory. Here Josie spent only one year, but an important one in his intellectual life.

His sister Ruth remembered that during this time "he first made friendships with schoolmates that became *comradeships*. They were few but they lasted through the years." A classmate, Nathan Newmark, named one such comrade as Jack Holmes, "dearest of all to Royce," but we know no more of Holmes except that he "went to sea." In spite of new friendships, Josie was not socially transformed, for Newmark described Royce in those days as "slight in figure, uncomely, red-headed, with pale face and prominent forehead; an omniverous reader, always with a book in his hand about school."

Newmark looked back on the school as "a rather stimulating place," a species of educational nirvana where older scholars worked with younger scholars, where projects and research abounded, a place "of spirited argument between keen lads and alert men on points of scholarship." The principal, Theodore Bradley, was a thoughtful man who daily assembled the boys in the auditorium and lectured them on history and "everything under the sun." Newmark thought the principal "intellectual, critical, hobbyish. His discipline lacked a proper perspective in values, but it stimulated analysis of facts. And he taught his foremost lesson most effectively—'Think for yourself.'" In English the boys read Shakespeare and enacted the parts, wrote weekly compositions, then memorized and recited them before the whole school. The mathematics instructor was a classicist from Trinity College, Dublin—tall, fat, and strict. In the gallery of the old church the boys learned Latin and Greek; in the basement a former pupil of Agassiz at Harvard taught chemistry and physics.

The school, which would be renamed Lowell, turned out a roster of distinguished graduates while Royce was there. Albert A. Michelson, the Nobel physicist, began his scientific career in that basement. There were future medical greats such as Joseph O. Hirschfelder, jurists such as Newmark, and politicians such as Frank Otis.

Still Royce himself provided the major stimulation for his own education. He learned of the Mechanics' Institute Library only a few blocks away on Post Street, a convenient stop on his way home from school. The fees were minimal ($1.50 per quarter), and its Renaissance-style three-story building included over seventeen thousand books. Its librarian, George C. Hurlbut, could direct a lad to Austen, Cooper, Dickens, Eliot, Hawthorne, Melville, Scott, and a host of others. If Josie looked for more serious enlightenment, there were Plato, Aristotle, Euclid, and Gibbon.

He recalls from these years his discoveries in literature and science that came like first loves to other boys. From the school library he devoured George Grote's multivolume *History of Greece*. Grote's work, which found the origins of democracy and freedom of thought in Athens, was later included by Royce among a score of epochal books in his life. In this period, too, he encountered Goethe's *Faust* and reveled in it "with the enthusiasm of personal discovery." That, his sister said, was true with much of his reading: "I recall his delight in the classics from which he would recite for the very joy of their resounding rhythm."

> If I should ever say to any moment:
> Tarry, remain:—you are so fair!
> Then you may lay your fetters on me,
> Then I will gladly be destroyed!
> Then they can toll the passing bell,
> Your obligations then be ended—
> The clock may stop, its hand may fall,
> And time at last for me be over!

Here was Faust speaking, not just to Mephistopheles, but to a lad in San Francisco. The preparations made in the woods of Avon Farm now vibrated to the romantic call.

> Happiness! Heart! Love! God!
> I have no name to give it!
> Feeling is everything,
> Name is but sound and smoke
> That damp celestial ardor.

Faust remained for Royce a favorite. Eleven years later he was calling it "the crown of modern poetic effort," "that epitome of the thought of our century."

Three decades afterward he could still remember his earliest philosophical development in these years, "when I used to wander about the streets of San Francisco at night speculating about the problem of life, and the eccentricities of human nature."

> My philosophic interests at this time, if I may dignify them by such a term, centered naturally about the problems of religion. I picked up my material everywhere, but chiefly I beleive [*sic*] from my inner consciousness. The amount of a priori system building I did in those days still makes my empiricist soul shudder.

In his reading, literature was always the handmaid of philosophy. Did we not know from his own words that he read novels from the Mechanics' Institute, we might infer the same from the stories he wrote in high school. Two of them still exist in his uneven scrawl, that product of a left-handed boy made into a right-handed penman. "A Nocturnal Expedition" tells of an Australian beach on which a first-person narrator dreams of watching another at "play with the old ocean's waves as they rolled in over the sand." The mood changes: "My mind was oppressed with a painful feeling of dread and I did not join with him in the sport." In the end the narrator is forced to watch his friend drown. Royce's somber side emerges, like his memory of a grave in the Grass Valley woods, and the story's setting is a curious prediction, for he would himself visit Australia under unhappy circumstances eighteen years later.

A more ambitious ten-page exercise was "The Miner's Grave," which extended the theme of death. We have already seen from this essay Royce's description of the area around Grass Valley and the deserted spot with a mound and a rough-hewn shingle to mark a grave. It is "the tale of a blighted heart," of a handsome, industrious, but reticent miner trying to make enough money to win the hand of his beloved. The girl and her family moved into town, which fact caused another miner, a shiftless gambler, to reform his ways and seek the hand of the young beauty too. But the former gambler remained rascal enough deliberately to mislead the industrious young man into believing his love had been false to him. Departing, the first suitor left a note: "I leave my claim to whosoever shall desire it, hoping that the gold he gains from it may not become as coals of fire to him, if he should find that through the faithlessness of One, his hopes of happiness should be like mine forever blasted." The young lady fell ill and died of consumption and was buried in the barren spot in the woods. The industrious young man consequently went mad, returned, and committed suicide over the grave. Here the narrator finds him. No coroner, "no medical skill could ever discover what I knew" as "I mourn over the occupant of the lonely grave."

The writing shows all the signs of one who read Scott and Tennyson and Dickens, maybe even Poe. The Mechanics' Institute offered him all those possibilities. And the story contains one detail which suggests an insight that Royce would vastly elaborate in his later writings. The first part of the tragedy takes place in 1851, "when a very few families had yet appeared in the town." The coming of a family—a gentleman, an old-maid sister, his daughter, and a little son—led to the reform of the reprobate gambler. Royce already understood through his mother the necessity of settled family life in the creation of community. Here as a boy in his early teens he was already using his past experience in his writing, including specifics from the Grass Valley years.

Equally important with his personal history and his romantic development was his further absorption in mathematics. He owned a copy of the 1869 edition of Elias Loomis's *Treatise on Algebra*, which took him through such topics as the properties of logarithms, Descartes's rule of signs, and Horner's method of incommensurable roots. Sam Hall, his Lincoln School chum who entered the high school with him, told of his friend astounding the mathematics teacher by covering in a few days the whole term's work in algebra and geometry. The teacher informed Royce that his "knowledge of mathematics far exceeded the teacher's, and that he need not do any further work in mathematics." So on his own Royce covered solid geometry, trigonometry, and logarithms, to and including quaternions. In his later list of the score of epochal books in his life, he included "two or three mathematical books in the M. I. Libr." It was not illogical that the boy, raised in a mining community and increasingly interested in mathematics, early chose an engineering career.

So Royce as a young teenager readied himself for an advanced intellectual life. Just before he died, he said that he already vaguely sensed his later interest in the community, both in Grass Valley and in these San Francisco school days. The community through which he walked every day from Folsom to Powell streets was growing rapidly in both size and complexity. The boy's move from Lincoln School to Boys' High School was itself an expansion of horizons, for the new walk or trolley ride took him beyond Market Street all the way up Powell to Sacramento Street. The route was a study of that complex modern community. From the unpaved, working-class environs of Folsom Street, he crossed the horse-drawn cars moving in "the slot" of Market Street and proceeded up

Powell past Union Square. Here he might well hear a labor organizer haranguing a group of unemployed workmen. If he did not turn down Post for an armload of books at the Mechanics' Institute Library, he could walk toward California Street and at one point look to the east into Chinatown. He might recall the sights and smells of the Grass Valley Chinatown, past and present standing side by side in his mind. But here the crowding of the Orientals was far more oppressive. Unemployed Chinese miners numbering over eleven hundred in 1870 flocked in from the goldfields, and most of the nearly ten thousand Chinese coolies who built the Central Pacific Railroad had by now drifted back unemployed to San Francisco. The Grass Valley Chinese were not nearly as segregated, but now with anti-Chinese feelings running high, with writers comparing them to "hibernating rattle-snakes" or "wallowing hogs," these in San Francisco were afraid to be found alone outside of Chinatown. If Grass Valley, the smaller community, moderately transcended ethnic lines, San Francisco, the larger, was rapidly failing. Yet the young Royce never evidenced the anti-Chinese feelings of his times.

The city was not only growing, it was differentiating itself. Wealth from the Nevada Comstock poured in. Barons such as James Flood were about to build intimidating palaces on Nob Hill, an area to which the Rincon Hill rich were already beginning to move. Nob Hill was also close to Royce's morning trek out of the working-class district, no more than a block or two if he turned his gaze west from Chinatown. Royce must have remembered the corresponding contrasts of rich and poor in Grass Valley—the cupolas and picket fences and manicured lawns of the mine managers sometimes only a stone's throw from the huts of the Cornish workers. In the Pussy Blackie story Royce included a pampered rich girl living in a palace. And in his later novel, a main figure, Alonzo Eldon, owned "a vast mansion on the great hill in San Francisco." He could add from experience, "Other millionaires were heaping up great houses on that hill."

Another young man walking the same streets of San Fran-

cisco that year would so deeply sense the discrepancies of rich
and poor that he engraved on the world of economics a vision
with which it wrestled for generations. Henry George's *Progress and Poverty* within a decade brashly proclaimed the breakdown of nineteenth-century communities as the rich grew
richer and the poor, poorer. A high school boy walking daily
from the poverty of Folsom Street, where his father peddled
fruit and his mother tended store, across Market into the bustling affluence of Powell Street in time carried a similar message couched in ethical terms to the field of philosophy.

CHAPTER 5

Berkeley Undergraduate

Not one youth of those so favoured, . . .
Came earnest as you came, resolved, like you,
To grasp all, and retain all, and deserve
By patient toil a wide renown like his.
Browning, *Paracelsus*

IN 1870 the library of the new University of California was unassuming. Located on the third story, at the top of Brayton Hall, it overlooked the outskirts of Oakland, a Jewish cemetery to the north, and the orchard of Samuel Merritt to the east. The thousand books were dog-eared and musty, pale old characters from another time and place. Few of the students (mostly men) at the new University of California climbed the flights of stairs. Generally commuters from San Francisco, the men had little incentive to stay around. On two days a week at four in the afternoon, all able-bodied male students were required to drill, marching down the dusty street as a uniformed battalion of the University Cadets. On those days they were free after morning classes, but most preferred to fill the intervening time with baseball or football rather than ascend to the thick coco-fiber matting of the library with its lonesome quiet.

One devoted exception was the boy who turned fifteen that November, Josiah, uncomfortable with the games below and delighted with the books above. After lunch he played chess—"this beautiful game," he called it, "the student's and the scholar's game." His opponent was usually another bookish student, Joseph Rowell, who became the university's librarian. The companionship was but a prelude to the hours when Josie sank into the silence of the room and the tumult of the printed

page. He remembered the library as ill accessible, uncata-
logued, hastily ordered, and poorly lighted (probably referring to the foggy days), but he looked upon the books "as
amongst the dearest friends of my youth." He recorded no
such fondness for the four o'clock donning of the cadet uniform and the mandatory march.

The University of California, beginning its second year of
classes, required military instruction because it was a Morrill
Act land-grant institution. The school's origins had been complicated. It was the reluctant offspring of a struggling academy
turned College of California and the state legislature's consti-
tutional requirement to establish a university. The final charter
of 1868 combined these two elements. Until 1872 it included a
preparatory program, the so-called fifth level, in which a student could enter without graduating from high school providing he or she was fourteen years or older and passed examinations in English grammar, arithmetic, geography, and United
States history. Eighty-seven students so registered with Royce
in 1870. Sarah must have been pleased at the prospect of thus
advancing her boy into the university, and young Josie would
have had no trouble with the examinations. So on September 22, 1870, not yet fifteen years of age, having completed only
one year of high school, he began his first term in the preparatory class of the University of California in Oakland.

The family simplified costs by moving over the bay with
him. If nothing else, that saved the five to eight dollars a week
students were then paying for board and lodging with private
families. The Royces found a house in the village of Brooklyn
across Dr. Samuel Merritt's lake from the new college. It was
not a bad time for a move across the bay, where they could
look back at what Royce would later call "the smoky city beyond the gray and chilly water." The Royce girls were beginning to leave home; all of them had prepared to teach, like
their mother, and they were either already or soon to be out
doing so. Besides, Sarah had loved the East Bay since her days
in Martinez, and the elder Royce's fruit wagon was in no sense
tied to crowded Folsom Street.

Josiah in college. Probably in his freshman year at the University of California, then in Oakland. The brass buttons are likely those of the University Cadets. (Courtesy of Nancy A. Hacker)

Brooklyn was a separate, unimpressive town. At this time it numbered about fifteen hundred people and included the ferry wharves, some cotton mills and small factories, the Tubbs Hotel, four churches, and a trotting racetrack, with farm-land everywhere nearby. For a nickel the horsecars took one from Brooklyn to downtown Oakland, a city of ten thousand people that grew in 1872 by annexing Brooklyn. In 1870 Oak-land boasted a public high school only a year old, a newly formed lake dammed by Dr. Merritt, and recently installed gas lights on downtown streets. Its subscription library became free and public in 1874 with Ina Coolbrith, the tall, luminously gray-eyed poet and universal mother of California literati, as librarian. Henry George came over from San Francisco to edit the *Oakland Transcript* after 1871, and before long he began writing *Progress and Poverty* there. Within a mile of Lake Mer-ritt was the countryside that Royce later described in his novel as having "groves of the dark eucalyptus-trees" and "large grain-fields."

Living at home insulated Josie from the shenanigans of his preparatory classmates. Their misconduct that winter caused the university's Academic Senate on three occasions to face "monitoring suitable discipline and supervision" of the pre-paratory class. The senate enjoined all faculty to report such students found in "public drinking places and in billiard sa-loons." In February five young men from the class were dis-missed. The senate decided to place the entire preparatory de-partment "on a military basis."

Josie's concerns were quite different. He now intended en-gineering, and we have seen how his skill in mathematics pointed in that direction. The Grass Valley years showed him some of the excitements and rewards of engineering in its min-ing guise. And his mother must have liked the idea, judging from her choice for him of books such as *The Miner Boy*. En-gineering was a solid and respectable ambition, calculated to furnish a productive and contributing member of society.

Other ideas, however, competed, and his degree goal was early overtaken by the arts and letters. The redirection must have begun with his maiden semester, perhaps in a course from William Swinton, the university's first and, at that time, only professor of English. Swinton, a dull teacher, friend of Henry George, and a man far more dedicated to the practical than the literary arts, also served as university librarian. Doubtless his observations of the young recluse in the library had something to do with Royce's grade in the course, a perfect 100. That first year he continued his algebra, and Paul Pioda, once principal of a young ladies seminary in Santa Cruz, taught him French. At Boys' High School in San Francisco, Royce had likely heard Pioda thump for the beauties of the French language; it contained, he said, "all the sounds of the rainbow." Pioda became an old familiar, for Royce studied French with him continuously till his senior year and then continued as his student for one term in Italian.

Josie's outside reading long paved the way for the humanities. Among the dozen or so books that most influenced his life, he listed novels from the Mechanics' Institute. And now to that same roster he added from the university library "an imposing copy of Homer." So the *Iliad* and the *Odyssey* sailed into his life even before he began his study of the classical languages three years later. When Royce was promoted to the regular freshman class in 1871, he transferred into the arts program in the College of Letters.

The college grew, expanding that year to 262 students, but more important to Josiah was the fact that the library swelled to three thousand volumes. In his year as a full-fledged freshman in the "fourth class," he continued his mathematics with William Welcker (a West Pointer who also taught military science) but added "belles-lettres" from Swinton, another English course, and ancient history.

On October 9, 1872, Royce's class on the Oakland campus boarded all the available horse-drawn vehicles, and singing and cheering, they paraded north on Telegraph Avenue to the fields and ravines of an area named Berkeley. They gathered around the foundations of two buildings and the flagpole of what was to be their future center. Uncultivated fields spread on all sides, with here and there a small orchard. The town numbered a few houses and perhaps only six businesses—a couple of saloons, including French Charlie's, a barbershop, and some stores. But on that October day the rising meadows among the oaks, two little streams, and the giddy view of the bay and Golden Gate were enough to excite anyone's imagination, particularly a young son of Argonauts whose mind was filled with Homer and Wordsworth.

In the fall of 1873 the university made the transition to its Berkeley campus, and Royce with it. The family had moved again, this time into Oakland proper on Washington Street between Lake Merritt and the Estuary. From here it was only a few short blocks to the south end of Telegraph Avenue, where Josie caught the "small horse car drawn by a single horse" north five miles to where the street butted into the new campus. The "one-horse, bob-tail" cars took an hour and a half to cover the six or seven miles between Oakland and Berkeley.

On the campus the flagpole and the two lonely buildings, now completed, stood stark in their clearings. North Hall, four stories of wood, embraced classrooms, an armory, and a faculty room, with "a sitting room or study for the young men" on the ground floor and a room for the young ladies two stories above. South Hall was of brick and iron and included high-ceilinged halls for instruction, several museums, and chemistry laboratories. On clear days from the tall corner window in the lecture room young Royce could see an unobstructed vista to the cluster of buildings rising around his old home across the bay. There were not many heads in the seats to interfere. Because of the move, the student body had fallen to 191, only 22 of whom were women. "The temporary difficulties in transit account for the falling off in number of young ladies," said the university *Register*. Conversely, the library at the north end of South Hall had grown. It now shelved over eleven thousand volumes in "brilliantly polished, black walnut bookcases" beneath "five bronze busts of ancient

Berkeley campus, 1874. The campus of the University of California
just after it moved with the young Royce from Oakland to the rural
hills of Berkeley. Old North Hall is the whiter building to the right;
Old South, to the left. The Bay and San Francisco are almost lost in
the fog. (Courtesy of the Bancroft Library, University of California,
Berkeley)

worthies." There were two tables and no more than thirty
chairs.

For all its primitive conditions, the Berkeley setting injected
a new spirit into the university; in a similar fashion, in contrast
with his previous diffidence and reticence, Royce now moved
into a period of assertion and self-confidence. His was the class
dubbed "crubstuffers," and in his junior year some of that
lightheartedness surfaced in the young man. He joined clubs
and came to be called Josh, instead of Josie. His name was
even associated with young ladies. 'They do say that Josiah,
our Josiah, has been flirting. Alas! . . . on whom can we depend? We thought that we could lay in a supply of pool on
Josiah, but the young lady acknowledges it." The student

columnists even alleged that Royce was making "mashes" on downtown Oakland's Broadway. The gibe could refer to ogling the girls or making conquests, but in all truth it is difficult to imagine either one.

In his senior year, so his son recalled, "he worked with pick and shovel and wheelbarrow grading the university grounds, earning $100.00." One student remembered such work as popular among the men, since it paid forty cents an hour. The labor, if he did it, and certainly the clubs and newspaper added a dimension of sociability, conventionality, perhaps even group solidarity that his days on Avon Farm and his lonely library vigils in San Francisco and Oakland had never allowed.

Two pictures of Royce, one taken in the early or mid-1870s, the other a few years later, show in the transition a less unruly mop of hair, more manly eyes and face, a nose and chin held a bit higher, somewhat more jauntily. John Clendenning calls it Royce's period of developing self-consciousness, a youth grasping for "some sense of the continuity between childhood and maturity." Royce himself wrote, "Youth means a flood of new sensations, of new emotions, of novel social stimulations, and of resulting vague ideals. The old self simply gets broken up." It was, he said, a grand part of life "because we young people evidently 'felt,' and were 'full of life,' and 'appreciated life'; while the older people were generally 'commonplace' and 'dull.'"

Did he dream of becoming a Phoebus Apollo? He composed a little piece about Mr. Phoebus Apollo visiting "an obscure province" called California, where the university included "some dandies whose pride I wish to lower." It would suggest that Josh's sociability was also restricted; there were some with whom he clearly felt no desire to mingle. Though his new openness may have stemmed from what he later considered one of youth's most compelling fears, becoming an outcast, still there were limits, and to be ostracized by a dandy was no disgrace. There was no call for loyalty to a false cause.

He wrote for the student newspaper, even for a few months in 1875 serving as one of its three editors. The first two editors represented the Durant Rhetorical Society and the Neolaean Society, but although Royce was a member of the latter, as an editor he represented "students not members of either society." At least thirty-five of his pieces appeared in the *Berkeleyan* during his senior year. For a time practically every issue carried something over his name—current prattle, university affairs, erudite reviews of established or recent authors. For three months he covered all the exchanges from other papers and journals. In his final year and particularly during his months as editor, his name appeared regularly in the campus gossip column, Collegiana. When he was teased with flirting ("the young lady acknowledges it"), the columnist added, "*Vale* Josiah, we will have to invest our shekels on Thad. Stevens," perhaps a reference to the womanizing of Senator Thaddeus Stevens of Pennsylvania. The next month the same column went on: "The fact is we did not make as much money on Thad Stevens as we anticipated. We have several pool tickets on California's favorite [Royce] which we will sell at a discount. Yes, we will sell them at a sacrifice. 90 *per cent* off."

It is harder to know what was meant when the wits declared it a lie that Josh "warms a whole pew in the Congregational Church." The Royce family at that time did attend the First Congregational Church in Oakland, judging from an old family hymnal that lists their pew as number 121, but did the young pundits consider it so ridiculous that Josiah would be found in a church? Or how much of a barb was in the reported scuttlebutt that "Royce intends to publish his oration on 'Truth in Art,' and that the President has promised to take one hundred copies." Was it thereby already understood that President Daniel Coit Gilman had a special confidence in young Royce? And were there deeper innuendos behind the joshings? How could the young editor not have ruffled feathers when he criticized his colleague's verse because "he thinks he has heard the first lines before, and secondly, because it has not that mellifulence [*sic*] which is always found in Greek epics."

More seriously, he editorialized on the relationship between one editor to the board of editors, which may be seen as a

Josiah, 1875. The college senior at the University of California, Berkeley. This year he wrote voluminously for the college paper, and was called Josh. (Courtesy of Nancy A. Hacker)

particular form of his larger lifetime query regarding the individual and the group. He covered campus affairs such as the problem of hazing, the emerging campus secret societies, and the need for a chess club (the game he loved). He both editorialized on and described the funeral of the university's first president, Henry Durant. He criticized John McCullough's interpretation of Hamlet at William Ralston's sumptuous new California Theater in San Francisco, because McCullough portrayed the Dane "with the impulsiveness of Othello," leaving out "the musing part of the original character." (The nunnery scene with Ophelia Royce found "simply electrical.") McCullough, an energetic actor with a booming voice, was just emerging from the shadow of his mentor, Edwin Forrest. McCullough's most sensitive acting years lay ahead, and young Royce undoubtedly perceived the situation rather well. He also commented on two conflicting reviews of Sir Henry Irving's London production of *Hamlet*. His literary criticism included pieces on George Eliot, Thomas Hardy, and Edgar Allen Poe, plus an essay on the nature of criticism itself.

The intellectual steam was rising for Josh, and these days marked not just the beginnings of a more loquacious, more communicative, more socially involved young man but a rapid development of his ideas and ideals. Remarkably, among the few hundred students in his small college, he observed the encroaching breakdown of common interests. He posed this tendency in terms of the countervailing pulls between the student's university and his or her class, forces that would someday become for his philosophy the world and the individual. On the embryonic campus he discerned members of the class knitted together "in a firm, life-long friendship that knows no distinction of wealth or social position." That was undeniably good. "Everywhere in the world when men are engaged in undertakings in which they feel a common interest, . . . a feeling of friendship always grows up among them which is the stronger, since each of two friends knows the weakness and strength of the other." But he also detected jealousies and quarrels between classes, around debating clubs, and over secret societies. The antidote to the divisiveness lay in a deeper appreciation that "all of us are where we are, whether in a better or worse condition than our neighbors, simply through the circumstances of the age in which we live and the particular agencies that have been at work upon us, and that, in consequence, there can be nothing in ourselves which gives us a superior right to that of any one else."

> He who feels how small a part he and his fellow atoms make of the great living, moving whole, Humanity, will appreciate how minute are all the distinctions of position in College when compared with the truly great ends of life, the bettering of knowledge, or the furthering of the advance of the whole race, a task in which each individual is but as a drop of water.

Responding to a letter to the editor that claimed science to be the superior branch of learning, Josh called the best scientist one whose questions led from natural science to life science to sociology to philology to history and on to literature. Literature and science are "fast friends, working for the one end of Human Advancement, twin sisters, who jointly rule as queens the Empire of Mind."

During his years in college Royce personally embodied his dictum that science and literature were joint queens of the intellect. President Gilman, whom Royce knew well by then, pictured such a wedding in his inaugural address to the university in 1872, emphasizing the West as a proper scene for the union. Royce never lost his interest in science and continued its study during his entire undergraduate years—physics, mechanics, geology, astronomy. Nevertheless he deplored some types of scientists—those who pitied "the benighted ignorance" of earlier knowledge and so were unable to enter into the spirit of another age. The ideal scientist has "a poet's power of sympathy, united with a historian's knowledge of facts." It was that kind of scientist he found in Joseph LeConte.

Royce idolized LeConte as "his greatest early inspiration." "The whole of my work," he said, would have been different "if my teacher had never spoken." LeConte was a Georgian who had left the practice of medicine to study with Louis Agassiz at Harvard. After the Civil War he abandoned the poverty of his Confederacy when he and his brother John, a physicist, accepted two of the first professorships in the new University of California. Joseph arrived in Oakland on the three-month-old transcontinental railroad, his enormous sloping forehead pushing his shaggy hair down and outward from his ears. He wore a full, curly beard and looked like the simian version of an Old Testament prophet, but his native grace and "gentleness of soul" endeared him to students. They called him "Joe," Royce explained, as an expression of affection "rather than of any lack of reverence." In his freshman year Royce could do no more than linger outside the door of LeConte's lecture room, catching only the modulated rhythms and inflections, but as a sophomore and for the rest of his years at Berkeley, he studied botany, geology, and natural science with LeConte.

In the years when Royce first knew him, LeConte moved reluctantly into support for the theory of evolution. Before he read Darwin, the scientist believed that "each species was introduced by the direct miraculous interference of a personal intelligence." He was and would remain a devoutly religious man. Now he began to compare evolution to the circulation of air and water, as in the formation and melting of glaciers, finding that each phenomenon leaves a residue that accumulates and results in changes. He compared species, too, with civilizations rising and falling but always providing "a residuum of ideas and principles" for what was to follow.

In such ways LeConte revealed the breadth of his thinking. Geologist, botanist, and chemist, he was above all a naturalist. A good friend of John Muir, the two men tramped the Yosemite, and it would be hard to say which man loved that glorious valley most. LeConte often had students in tow, and perhaps on some occasion (we have no direct evidence) young Royce may have been included. In the Yosemite LeConte first posed to himself serious questions about Darwinian change. That forested, stream-laced, glacial valley, too, caused him to stand and literally weep in the presence of its natural beauty. The company of this man, if only in the fields and meadows of Berkeley, permitted Royce the emotional recall of his own tramps through the woods at Avon Farm, his own first appreciation of wilderness. At the same time LeConte gave him both insights into the significance of evolutionary theory and an appreciation for "the architecture of an argument." For Royce, LeConte was "a beginning of philosophy."

On the literary side of his intellectual development, he continued to champion fiction. In his junior year he earned a first prize for his Charter Day oration extolling the modern novel, an influence that has "moulded our destiny." In the novel's direct appeal to our feelings, in its turn away from majestic Promethean subjects to "the internal struggles and triumphs" of a common man like Jean Valjean, it held new powers for changing individuals and thus reforming society. To prove his point, he chose George Eliot's *Mill on the Floss*, not because it was dramatically or artistically superior to *Adam Bede* or *Middlemarch*, but because it best illustrated "the instructive influence a novel may exercise." For much of the story we are engrossed in the "uneventful childhood of a simple English country girl," swept up eventually in the power of a natural disaster. Deep moral lessons are inseparably intertwined with the artistic effects. It thus becomes a culmination of what contemporary fiction attempts: "to view things as they really are, and to subject them all to law" while at the same time applying the highest human questions to the tawdriest human lives. "As Vulcan wrought beauty on the shield of Achilles," so the modern novel carries on the traditions of literary art by asking great questions of simple things.

In his attraction to George Eliot one can make out faint reflections of Royce's own life. Many of Eliot's characters, such as Maggie in *Mill on the Floss* or Dorothea in *Middlemarch*, were sensitive souls struggling to find themselves in uncongenial surroundings. As a child, Maggie, like Josie, chose the inward life, just as Dorothea in her marriage chose a selfless devotion to the intellect over romantic love. Dorothea desired to restructure the villages for the workingman, and her effort at communal reform reflected Eliot's and many Victorians' concern with the plight of traditional beliefs and values in a fragmented, complex society. Eliot's response was to assert a community of feeling, a unification through sentiment, in the spirit of Wordsworth, a favorite poet of both Eliot and Royce. For Eliot the portrayal of the common person, like the poor weaver Silas Marner, taught her readers to feel the universal elements in the slow reconciliation with an estranged community. Women were the particular intruments of this communality—Dorothea and Maggie, Dolly Winthrop in *Silas Marner*—while the men, like Tom in *The Mill* or Bulstrode in *Middlemarch*, were involved with the contrary world of business and politics. Royce must have understood this especially when he considered his own mother's early life in California.

Royce remained a devotee of Eliot's novels, in tune with her and even with her paramour, George Henry Lewes, whom he also reviewed enthusiastically for the *Berkeleyan*. In Lewes's *Problems of Life and Mind*, Royce had read a similar message: "While thinking men appear, on a superficial view, to be daily separating wider and wider from each other, they are, on a deeper view, seen to be drawing closer together,—differing in opinion, they are approximating in spirit and purpose."

If LeConte was Royce's guiding mentor in the sciences, Edward Rowland Sill, the poet and critic, became his torchbearer in literature. Royce seems to have taken very little, if any, formal course work with Sill, but during his last year he nevertheless considered this man of "delicate and fertile literary fancy" to be a vital influence on his life.

Sill as an undergraduate at Yale knew President Gilman as a librarian there. The young New Englander, after graduating from Yale, sailed to California on a *Wanderjahr*. In Sacramento as a post office clerk, he felt himself a pilgrim and a stranger "out here in heathendom." He moved for two years to the Sierra foothills at Folsom ("a gross, deadening place"), where "a few respectable, good, vulgar people, . . . keep up a Sunday School, make a sparse gathering of audience around the empty

church Sundays, and try to build up a new New England out
here." This was ten years after Sarah and Josiah Royce lived
in Folsom, and judging from Sill, not much had changed.
Though he made good friends in California, he wrested himself from the land of "Pike's, fools, fools, fools, and other
fools" and went east to study divinity at Harvard. After writing for a New York newspaper and teaching school in Ohio,
still only thirty years old, he returned to his friends in California as the Oakland High School principal. Gilman, then president of the university, came to appreciate Sill's poetry and essays and in 1874 brought him to Berkeley to succeed the
farmer-oriented Swinton as professor of English.

Sill's thin, carefully bearded, handsome face with piercing
eyes, his bodily grace and charming manner automatically won
him admirers. In Berkeley he rode a black horse around the
campus and into the hills, where "the twilight poet," like
LeConte and Royce, would relish the magnificent views of
the bay.

> And I am glad that neither golden sky,
>   Nor violet lights that linger on the hill,
>   Nor ocean's wistful blue shall satisfy,
>   But they shall fill
> With wild unrest and endless longing still
> The soul whose hope beyond them all must lie.

Sill set high standards in the teaching of English, probably
one reason Royce liked him so much. All students of English
should simultaneously concentrate during their four years on
the history and structure of the language, past and present
literature, and composition, rhetoric, and criticism. The com-
parative languages recommended were Anglo-Saxon, Latin,
Greek, German, and French, as well as English. All of these
Royce embarked upon during these years, with the final ap-
proval, if not the direct tutelage of Sill.

To Royce, Sill was galvanic. Nearly twenty years later when
the poet was dead, Royce wrote about their relationship: "I
knew him well; he was first a valued teacher and adviser of my
own, and afterwards an intimate friend." A "peculiarly sensi-

tive" man, Sill, in Royce's eyes, had "a fearless, devoted, and generous heart."

Once I found him very gloomy. His work at Berkeley was wearing him out, and certain of his worst pupils . . . had just been paining him by bitter speeches and cruel misunderstandings. I gossiped on about the affair to him, in an irresponsible way, of course, until among other things I said: "You see, Sill, all this comes from your determined fashion of casting pearls before swine. Why will you always do it?"—"Ah, Royce," he responded, with a perfectly simple and calm veracity in his gentle voice, "you never know in this world whether you were really casting pearls at all until you feel the tusks."

This is the way Royce saw Sill's message: "Science is, or ought to be, poetry, and poetry is knowledge, and the humanity of the future will not divide life but will unite it." It was a mission to bridge Royce's joint queens of the intellect, and as an apostle against specialization Sill enlisted young Royce for the duration of his life.

Already Royce was a philosopher, a romantic figure walking alone the wild hills of Berkeley. LeConte and Sill might teach and question, leading him with Plato out of the cave of shadows, but Royce was reaching beyond. "The true kingdom of learning," he said later, "like the kingdom of heaven, is within you." Looking within, he was finding bothersome questions based on troublesome observations. As a sophomore, age seventeen, he had seen the contradictions in the human being: "a ferocious lamb, a revengeful dove, an herbivarous [sic] tiger." Do not trust appearances, he was saying. And in his own life, "I felt confident, and helpless, all at once." Now was youth's search for "power, courage, plan, and above all social status,— a place among the 'men my brothers,—men the workers.'" Selfhood demands independence, and it forces philosophical questions about truth and reality. In the flyleaf of his notebook he inscribed lines from one of Goethe's late poems, "Selige Sehnsucht" (Blessed Longing):

> *Und so lang du das nicht hast*
> *Dieses: Stirb und werde!*

Bist du nur ein trüber Gast
Auf der dunklen Erde.
[Till by this you be possessed:—
Die and have new birth!
You are just a sombre guest
On the darkened earth.]

In his senior year he won a prize in speaking for his "Truth in Art" (Gilman was supposed to have ordered one hundred copies!), defeating William Carey Jones, a future friend. That year San Francisco's prestigious *Overland Monthly* accepted one of his earliest philosophical essays, "The Life-Harmony." The publication must have pleased him, for a poem of his idol Edward Rowland Sill preceded his essay, and in the same issue was verse of his librarian in Oakland, Ina Coolbrith.

Does human development, he asked, flow "steadily onward, undisturbed by the violent surface action of events," or does it move in "tremendous convulsions," as in human history or animal evolution? Hegel, he admitted, would say that the spirit progresses "by very dint of conflict" and uneven struggle. But Royce disagreed. "The mind of man is not a comet wandering from system to system in orbits of incalculable eccentricity." Historians (as he had said of scientists) engage in that fallacy when they feel superior to the past and do not see common tendencies and essential unities. "The strongest tie that can be mentioned as binding together the race is the fact of common sensibilities and common emotions, and the most certain and universally intelligible proof of this is found in art, and especially in poetry." The ancient Greeks erred in setting themselves superior to the barbarians; it should be harder for us to fall into such ethnocentricity because we can see how their poetry and drama inspire grand universal thoughts, even though their gods have passed into fable. The person who can see these unities, whether or not he can "determine the chemical constitution of the sun," is at heart "in sympathy with the race, with the humanity that has ever been content to suffer that it might grow nobler, to be lonely that it might find love, to long that it might be satisfied." "As we have learned the brotherhood of races, let us learn the brotherhood of the ages also."

Both his senior thesis and the oration he was chosen to deliver at commencement deal with classical and philosophical themes: the first with Prometheus, the second with Antigone. How could a religious man like Aeschylus exalt the rebel Prometheus over the supreme God, Zeus, who becomes the villain? Royce answers that Zeus here represented not the holy God but the terror and brutishness in human nature. Likewise Antigone justifiably defied King Creon and buried her brother because she inherited a morality independent of the law. Her independence was her humanity, and through it she infused art with the unity of all history and all human experience. For a young man about to embark on what he called "a stormy sea," the ocean of philosophy, independence was not just a right but a mark of humanity and the unity of all spirit.

The last days in Berkeley were warm and exciting. The joshings he had received in the *Berkeleyan* columns persisted in the students' bogus commencement program. Here he was portrayed as a fiery-haired Jehovah and a swelled head with a capacious stomach. Under the title "Juggler Royce" he was:

> Wide mouth—mule ears—pug-nose—red hair,
> Style, anything but *debonair*;
> Although a regular Chinese *Josh*,
> He'll treat you to some classic bosh.
>   He comes—he comes—grave as a pall,
> With tones dry as a summer drouth;—
>   Good God! Is that a hole in the wall?
> Oh, no! He's opening his mouth!

But these quips seem not to have infected his own spirit. He delivered an oration before the class of 1875 and kept a handwritten copy until the day he died. "Friendship, gentlemen [this was the last year that the graduating class had no women members], enduring, firm, noble friendship is the best of man's possessions in this world of change. . . . In life's wintry storms it ever provides a refuge. Life's spring mornings are made happier by its presence." Sentimentally rhetorical, "all his unfledged geese were swans," and he was closing his formative period of life in California. He had made his mark. Twelve years later the class historian wrote of "that big red head—that first caused us to laugh, then to respect it, and finally to be proud of it as a class trophy." Another classmate looked back over half a century and concluded, "Of those who were connected with the University in my time, the two persons whose individuality impressed itself most forcibly on my mind were Joseph LeConte, professor of geology, and Josiah Royce, a member of my class."

Daniel Coit Gilman observed Royce all through that last year, heard his winning orations, and read his pieces in the *Berkeleyan*. For many years he would be the young man's patron and began by persuading several San Francisco businessmen, whose names have not survived, to support Royce in European study. The recipient could expect about one thousand dollars. Royce wrote Gilman that with his own health and hopefulness, the stipend would be "the making of my whole life." Gilman himself was off to Baltimore to the new Johns Hopkins University, where he made his greatest contribution to American higher education. Sill's "Departure of the Pilot" included lines that surely suggested Royce's feelings about Gilman and could have been a prophecy.

> But upon our voyage far
> We shall meet in other days,
> Since the same pure polar star
> Shines to beacon both our ways.

Once again, Royce had been involved with beginnings, with seminal times. He, with a small band of teachers and scholars, walked the virgin campus of an emerging institution. Both Grass Valley and San Francisco provided parallel face-to-face experiences, and they were continued in Berkeley. His sister probably reflected his own comments when she called his university years "golden days . . . when numbers were small enough for faculty and students to touch hands and hearts, and intellects grew keener, 'as iron sharpeneth iron.'"

"Remember how narrow was the world," he exclaimed to a later class at Berkeley. But it was wide enough to give him another version of what community might be, and it was creative enough to free him from his inward shyness. Above all, it left him knowing what he wanted to do with his life. Before such a time, as his friend Sill wrote, "The soul's flight is only the haphazard fluttering of an insect,—afterward, it is the swift, sure flight of the bird, that seeks its own tree-top and sings upon its way."

CHAPTER 6

First Flight

No more you are held in capture
Darkly over-shadowed waiting,
You anew are torn by rapture
Upwards to a higher mating.
    Goethe, "Selige Sehnsucht"

"WHEN a youngster will talk metaphysics the best thing to do with him is to shut him up by himself, or find some place where the people are as mad as he." That was one way Royce later saw the predicament of a budding philosopher in California. President Gilman, who knew Royce well, recognized the better of those two alternatives—a more expansive, if not more mad, environment. Pilgrim needed to confront the world with all its bright snares and dark raptures. So Gilman not only arranged the money for Josiah's first flight beyond the borders of California, but he also armed the young man with letters of introduction to Easterners along the way.

The transcontinental railroad framed his pioneer departure from home and his earliest glimpse of the East, like Pussy Blackie reversing Sarah Royce's trek. He must have thought of his mother's wagon stories as he stared from the cars at the passing plains. Only four years before, Robert Louis Stevenson buddied up for soap, towel, and a board to stretch between the seats; Royce, too, must have gone the cheapest way. No matter. He was young. He bore no illness as did Stevenson. And his spirit soared at the prospect of moving from the raw lecture halls and cramped libraries of California to the established intellectual centers of the world.

Late summer of 1875 in Boston, he sat in his only, threadbare suit at a dinner party with some dozen others, mostly in evening dress. George Dorr was his host, a young businessman, son of Mary Ward Dorr, socialite of Boston and Cambridge, introduced to Royce by Gilman. The story is told of Dorr, already dressed for dinner, opening the door for the young Westerner in his frayed clothes, saying something gracious about Royce being correct, it was too hot for formal wear, and quietly disappearing upstairs to change his own suit.

William James was there, probably in proper dress. It was the first meeting of Royce and James. If ever there are times in a life when the whole future is wrapped in the germ of a moment, this was indeed such a time—the beginning of a forty-year friendship that ultimately would influence the course of American thought. We do not know what they talked about that first night, but pressed, James later remembered "the charm and delight" of Royce's conversation. If that description was correct, it is another sign of the leap Josiah made from the shy, introverted boy of Grass Valley and San Francisco. It was a social jump, too, dining in the homes of the wealthy, not just writing fanciful stories about them. In Grass Valley terms, the nineteen-year-old son of an itinerant fruit peddler now found his way through the avenue of education into the houses of mine owners. The significance of dinner at the Dorrs, however, would not be evident for many years. First, the Westerner tasted Europe.

Royce's choice of Germany for study is puzzling from a personal viewpoint, since he was much better prepared in the French language, and England would have been a return to his family roots. But in other respects Germany was a logical preference. Kant and Hegel established Germany as the heartland of philosophical thinking. For over half a century it attracted a steady stream of Americans in theology, engineering, and literature. There was even an undefinable rapport between the American West and Germany. It provided the training for the elite of the mining engineers, such as James Duncan Hague, Louis Janin, Charles Rueger, and William Pettee, all western engineers who had studied in Germany. There were six or seven Californians alone studying engineering at Freiburg in 1867. They were welcomed by a land in love with the American frontier; western writers, especially Bret Harte and Mark Twain, were in great vogue in the Germany of the 1870s and 1880s. By that time over two thousand American students were enrolled in German universities. How many were from the American West, we cannot say, but in time Westerners such as Gifford Pinchot, John R. Commons, Richard T. Ely, George Pardee, Philip Sheridan, and the future rancher Theodore Roosevelt would all have student contacts with Germany. One apt parallel was a western intellectual, Lincoln Steffens, who fourteen years later enthusiastically departed Berkeley, as Royce had, and headed for Germany to study philosophy. Down a similar path would go George Holmes Howison, Berkeley's first professor of philosophy, who described a "strange sense of long-cherished hopes at length fulfilled" when he found himself "actually within the fatherland of Lessing and Goethe and Schiller, of Leibnitz and Kant and Fichte and Hegel."

Royce remembered his generation dreaming "of nothing but the German University. . . . German scholarship was our master and our guide." It was cheap, too. Study in Germany, including travel, would average about a third of the cost of a year at an eastern school. The subvention Josh received was a sufficiency.

After his visitations in the East came his maiden sea voyage from New York to Hamburg aboard a new, iron ship, the German steamer *Klopstock*, whose very name must have excited him with its poetic connotations. He surely loved the voyage. For the rest of his life he would resort to a sailing journey when in need of relaxation or recreation. Three months followed in Heidelberg, where the nineteen-year-old learned to be comfortable with a foreign language and a foreign culture. He probably read James Morgan Hart's *German Universities*; most American students bound for Germany used it as a guide. Hart, like Royce, reserved a few months on arrival to tackle "that Gibraltar ycleped the German language." It was not too rugged a chore for Royce; he dropped the special exercises sooner than intended and went straight to lectures. Thereby he gained more time to take advantage of Hart's advice on cigars and pipes, coffee and beer, choice of accommodations, and the warning against epithets such as *dummer Junge* (unless one wished to defend himself in a duel). Royce felt much like Hart: "I was in the spring-time of life, unfettered, free to follow the promptings of fancy, and, above all, stimulated by the consciousness that daylight had at last dawned upon my studies."

In September Daniel Gilman, traveling through Europe recruiting his first faculty for Johns Hopkins University and talking with men such as James Bryce, Leopold von Ranke, and Herbert Spencer, dropped in on his student from Berkeley. The two former Californians, the president and his erstwhile undergraduate friend, spent the day enjoying the countryside. They probably walked. Hart recommended walking in Germany; everyone did it for pleasure, and there were no "roughs" as in America to disturb the peace. "Every village and by-path and *Garten* became a familiar haunt."

Students, according to Hart, lived in rooms scattered through the town, each, no matter how poor, having a study and sleeping room to himself. "Chumming" was unknown. "The superiority of the German system is incalculable; it is more manly, it conduces to independence of study and prevents much waste of time."

As the opening of the term approached in October, Royce, without having enrolled at Heidelberg, moved to Leipzig. It was not unusual. Students transferred freely from university to university. Their good standing in any one entitled them to admission in any other, so they shopped around for professors and lectures.

At Leipzig Royce matriculated, which meant that he presented himself with his degree documents, paid his fees (about five dollars), and received his student card for the faculty of philosophy, inscribed "Herr Josiah Royce aus Grace Valley." Though hardly an accurate transcription of his home, the young man was still identified by the California goldfields,

Josiah in Germany, 1876. A youthful Royce (twenty-one years of age), but a young man whose serious demeanor betokens a mind that mastered German in a matter of months to the level of hearing and discussing abstract philosophical lectures.

not by San Francisco or Oakland. University students enjoyed unique privileges, and the card admitted "Josiah Royce
aus Grace Valley" almost anywhere, reduced his meal and
drinking costs, and even protected him from arrest by the local
police.

Royce heard five courses that winter, including Wilhelm
Windelband's lectures on Greek philosophy, but Wilhelm
Wundt was the chief attraction that brought him to Leipzig.
Royce signed up for two of his lectures in anthropology and
logic. To Gilman he wrote that in Wundt "I have a thoroughly
live man, and one who will quite possibly make a powerful
impression on the thought of the next decade or so, for he is
still in his younger prime."

Wundt was indeed destined to become a landmark in the
emerging field of experimental psychology, divorcing the subject field from theology and morality and seeking "facts, nothing but facts." Lincoln Steffens, depressed by the deadening
work in Wundt's laboratory, lashed out against the professor:
"His Logic is untenable, his ethics commonplace, his system
absurd or childish." But Royce, ten years earlier, learned much
from Wundt—the uses of empirical psychology and the values
of experiment and experience. He would incorporate Wundt's
approaches in his first philosophical essays on mind and sense
data and later in his concept of the community as a coherent,
concrete person.

The next term Royce moved to Göttingen. "I have a strong
desire," he wrote Gilman, "to hear [Rudolf Hermann] *Lotze*, . . .
a professor who seems generally acknowledged as the first in
constructive philosophy now living in Germany. He also has
done much in Psychology, but his school is more traditionally
German than Wundt's, and certainly with more of the Idealistic tendency in it."

Hart also took a course from Lotze, "a general speculative
discussion of the laws of the material world in their relations
to the human spirit, something between physics and psychology." He found the professor interesting, but Hart cut the
course "rather shabbily." It is doubtful that Royce ever missed

a lecture. Lotze brought Royce head-on with post-Kantian idealism and a systematic overreaching philosophy. He was the single most important philosophical influence that Royce brought back from Germany. The student expected to "never forget nor disregard" Lotze's lectures. But Germany did more than this for Royce. It intensified all of his scholarly tendencies. If in his last year at Berkeley he had relaxed somewhat, even making "mashes" on Broadway, he did not therefore abandon his serious reading and writing. In Germany a similar ability to play life to the full seems to have continued. "The French university," said Matthew Arnold, "has no liberty, and the English universities have no science; the German universities have both." But Arnold concluded that the aim in Germany is "to encourage a love of study and science for their own sakes." That certainly happened to Josiah.

We do not know precisely how much Royce socialized, but there is no reason to doubt that he drank beer and smoked cigars. Somewhere in his early years he became an inveterate smoker, and perhaps it was in Germany. Still, the lecture rooms—cheerless, unattractive, dingy, with hard benches and close air—generated his greatest excitement. "One went to Germany," he wrote, 'still a doubter as to the possibility of the theoretic life; one returned an idealist, devoted for the time to pure learning for learning's sake, determined to contribute his *Scherflein* [bit] to the massive store of human knowledge." The ideal of painstaking scholarship, abstract and theoretical, guided him like a grail through the rest of his life. He was always able to mitigate that ideal with something of practical, present-minded freshness, tendencies that he may have brought with him from the American West; but Germany overlaid his life with a true scholarly method that he never lost.

Whether Germany would also mask his western roots to the point of suppression is another question. Many thoughtful commentators on his philosophy have considered it so. For example, George Herbert Mead, subsequently his devoted disciple, ultimately doubted the American applicability of his ideas, believing that he had grafted another culture onto his origins. There is some truth to this argument, but as we will see, the superstructure never really concealed the foundations.

The German academic patina was recognized especially by Gilman, astute as he was in ferreting out and nurturing promising young men, and it was that friend from Berkeley who provided Royce with the opportunities for similar development. Poking through the intellectual centers of Europe for his new faculty, Gilman explained to prospective professors that the vision of graduate research guiding his new Johns Hopkins University required a company of bright, promising, carefully selected young scholars, to be called fellows. This group of junior savants eventually included Thorstein Veblen, John Dewey, Frederick Jackson Turner, and Charles Shinn. Among the first year's twenty-one, Gilman chose Josiah. He thereby joined, as the university's historian put it, "a more remarkable group of college graduates than had ever before gathered for study anywhere in America."

Except for finances, Royce would have liked to stay in Germany another year, but in September 1876, with a few boxes of books and some German periodicals to follow by mail, he arrived in Baltimore, once more to join a newborn and trailblazing university.

The success of Gilman's vision for Johns Hopkins depended wholly on his choice of the six professors, the few associates, and the little band of fellows. Those tapped would rear an institution dedicated to research and offering only the Ph.D., a degree almost unknown in America. Around the Baltimore site at Howard and Monument streets, the tone of Germany was not difficult to sense. And it lay not only in the curriculum and the research-oriented doctorate. Royce with four other fellows and two associates organized a German Club (a *Kneipe*), a "frugal symposia," where every week they gathered at a restaurant to speak German, drink beer, eat a few crackers and cheese, smoke, and talk about their work and the real world.

New colleges, properly led and funded, are peculiarly rich environments for intellectual growth. Departments and disciplinary demands are weak enough to permit frequent contacts across those lines, and if the involved minds are young and flinty, the sparks inevitably fly. Johns Hopkins was an especially charged spot, for not even undergraduates were around to disturb these prodigies from energizing one another. Even among the fellows, disciplinary concentrations were sparse. Shades of California, Royce did not have a trained philosopher to guide him. Instead fellows were encouraged to lecture one another and stir up reaction; Royce quickly responded with two series on Schopenhauer and Kant.

Instruction revolved around seminars, then termed seminaries. Typical of German universities, they covered broad areas of study and met regularly to hear and discuss papers. The first and chief of these, the Seminary on History and Politics, was organized by Herbert Baxter Adams, himself a product of Heidelberg. In it Royce read a paper on Spinoza, but he listened to and debated several papers that must have intensified his interest in the subject of community, carrying forward the floating ideas and impressions from his Grass Valley experience. Herbert Baxter Adams talked on early village communities, developing his Teutonic germ theory of history, tracing the embryos of American democratic institutions back to the forests of medieval Germany, where councils emerged among the tribes and gave their assent by brandishing spears. Henry C. Adams reported on cooperating societies. Albert Shaw studied the history of Amana, the intensely communal religious *Gemeinschaft* that settled in Iowa in the 1850s.

This Adams seminar developed a tradition of interesting work on community, and only a few years later produced a work that would also influence Royce. In 1884 a young Californian, Charles Howard Shinn, later a friend of Royce and the brother of Milicent, the editor of the *Overland Monthly,* reported on his thesis, "Mining Camps: A Study in American Frontier Government." His director described it as "a veritable mine in the study of frontier law and of the wonderful evolution of self-government in California mining camps, where old Saxon forms of associated families of *men* sprang full armed into life and law." When Royce wrote his own history of California, he leaned heavily on Shinn's work, which must have carried special weight for him because of its Baltimore imprimatur.

Other Westerners besides Royce and Shinn tasted of Herbert Baxter Adams and were less impressed. Thorstein Veblen came from Wisconsin in 1881, and in the seminar presented a paper that included commentary on land booms in the American West. But Veblen in no sense followed the germ theory and in fact left Hopkins unhappily that same year.

Twelve years after Royce, the Adams seminar would cause another young western student, Frederick Jackson Turner, to rebel against the whole germ theory and transplant the roots of American democracy from Teutonic lands into his own American West. Royce's writing predated Turner in emphasizing the critical importance of the western experience, and we will see how Royce's history stood between the theories of Adams and Turner, thus linking two of the products from the Johns Hopkins world of ideas.

Baltimore, however, embodied more than work and thought. There were evenings of beer and cigars with the German Club. His friendship with Gilman deepened in frequent visits to the president's house, where he sat by the fire and played with the cat. There Royce met another of Gilman's protégés, Charles Lanman, a classicist fresh from three years in Germany. Lanman enrolled in Royce's course on Schopenhauer, and when Lanman proposed a course in Sanskrit, Royce was one of five who enrolled. Josiah often thereafter addressed Lanman as "Dearest Guru." Since the two eventually taught together at Harvard and lived close by in Cambridge, Lanman became one of Royce's closest friends.

There was time, too, for literature. Royce was part of a club dedicated to the art of writing novels. They read Charlotte Brontë and Thackeray and, of course, George Eliot. Royce enjoyed the leader, an unnamed New York writer, and long afterward remembered the meetings, the talks, the late night departures. "They were golden evenings, those, when we played with life as children with soap-bubbles, and enjoyed life as birds do a crystal mountain lake."

Baltimore was itself a social education for Royce. There was the unfamiliar environment of southern culture, with its aristocratic traditions often reflected in the theaters, art galleries, and museums. Above all, Royce came to know the delightful family of George Buchanan Coale, a businessman from an old Maryland family. One of Coale's two sons was a student at the University of Maryland, and his daughter, Mary, would become a special friend. John Clendenning feels that the Coales personified the qualities of settled status that Josiah's life had so lacked. Certainly the Maryland family were eastern gentility; their rootedness contrasted sharply with the social dynamism of his unsettled California childhood.

Taken all in all—the excitement of intellectual involvement, the seminary, the German Club, the literary talk, the culture of the South, the numbers of friends—it is not surprising that Royce remembered these years in metaphors suggesting the revolutionary generation of his beloved Wordsworth: "a dawn wherein ''twas bliss to be alive' . . . [in which] one longed to be a doer of the word, and not a hearer only, a creator of his own infinitesimal fraction of a product, bound in God's name to produce it when the time came."

He spent the summer of 1877 in Boston and Cambridge, enjoying the Boston Public, the Athenaeum, and the Harvard libraries; raising a little money, it is presumed, by working as a gardener in Harvard Yard; and, above all, renewing his acquaintance with William James. In contrast with the earlier dinner at the Dorrs, Royce felt the friendship really began on a summer day in the James house on Quincy Street when Josiah "was permitted to pour out my soul to somebody who really seemed to believe that a young man might rightfully devote his life to philosophy if he chose." Considering the paucity of opportunities for a life work in philosophy, his friends, even at Johns Hopkins and certainly in his western years, had advised him to let the subject alone. James, in contrast, confirmed him as one of those souls "who ought to be able to find themselves in their own way." If, Royce said later, people criticize James for being too fond of cranks, "Well, I am one of James's cranks. He was good to me, and I love him. The result of my own early contact with James was to make me for years very much his disciple."

The Johns Hopkins fellowship was renewed, and Royce spent a second year in Baltimore. He was excited that James came down from Harvard as a visiting professor offering a ten-lecture course in psychology, "The Senses and the Brain and Their Relation to Thought." Royce signed up, of course, even though he was by then well into the writing of his doctoral dissertation. James was still a physiological psychologist, and the great philosophical debates betweeen James and Royce lay ahead, but the friendship was growing.

The title of Royce's dissertation, "Of the Interdependence of the Principles of Knowledge: An Investigation of the Problems of Elementary Epistemology," suggests how specialized was the inquiry. Even the repetition five times in one title of the preposition "of" conveys how little Royce was seeking a general audience. The thesis discussed the pragmatic effects of theory and practice on knowledge or truth; the same judgment may be true at times, at others not, depending on the purpose. The theme was a long cry from the future Roycean absolutism, yet there were some predictions of things to come. In his conclusion he asked: "Which is prior, impersonal or personal Consciousness? For to this we answer, Individual Consciousness is but a shadow; what is permanent is the World." Through what this foreshadows of his later *World and the Individual*, it is clear that the scholar was on a particular metaphysical path. President Noah Porter of Yale, a philosopher, was drafted to read the thesis and help examine him. "The examination was fair, but lengthy—all full of such requirements as: Give some account of Spinoza's doctrine of God and World; or of Plato's Dialogues; or of Aristotle on time, space, matter, motion, and the infinite; etc."

So it was that on June 13, 1878, at the age of twenty-two, he was awarded the Ph.D. degree by Johns Hopkins during a

commencement in which the new university's first four doc-
torates were granted. Basil Gildersleeve, the classicist, once a
wounded Confederate soldier and later Hopkins's first professor, spoke of the trials through which the students had been
put. He claimed that the degrees were granted "not only for
knowledge acquired but for the spirit manifested—that spirit
'which counts nothing done while aught remains to be done.'"

Much in Royce's life did remain to be done. For one thing,
he had no job. Gilman hoped to find a place for him at Yale,
but nothing came. Finally on July 1 an offer arrived from the
University of California. Berkeley again! And the job was only
an assistantship in English! It did, however, pay $1,200 a year;
he was in debt to both Lanman and Gilman ("I am as poor as
one wants to be"); there was some unspecified prospect of
teaching a bit of philosophy; and besides, there were no other
possibilities. He felt like an "insignificant foam-crest among
the world-waves."

It was on that level of enthusiasm that he boarded the train
in New York. With an introduction in hand from Gilman, he
quieted his bitter feelings, took advantage of the trip, and
stopped in St. Louis to visit William Torrey Harris, a dynamic
Connecticut Yankee who before the Civil War as a disciple of
Bronson Alcott, Goethe, and Coleridge brought his brand of
transcendentalism to the Mississippi frontier. There he gathered a group of western intellectuals intent on studying Hegel
and applying idealism to frontier American conditions. One
of them, Henry Brokmeyer, lived like Thoreau in a hut in the
Missouri woods. Harris and Brokmeyer and forty-nine other
charter members formed the St. Louis Philosophical Society
in 1866. They published the first and at that time the only
philosophical publication in America, the *Journal of Speculative
Philosophy,* which became the vehicle that would introduce to
the emerging professional world of philosophy such lights as
William James, Charles Sanders Peirce, John Dewey, and, very
early, the young Royce. The new doctor of philosophy found
his talk with Harris "a very interesting interview." The journal's editor accepted Royce's article on Schiller for publication.

On westward, he traced the trail of his parents, but in cars made famous by Robert Louis Stevenson—the Plains, the Rockies, down Weber Canyon in the Wasatch, the bleached deserts, the "breath-checking sublimity" of the Sierras, "all now impressed on my memory as they were not previously." He found his home in Oakland "peaceful and happy, my Mother unchanged and as well-pleased to meet me as mothers usually are under such circumstances, my Father in poor health, but full of welcome for me." But the feelings expressed in his last letter to William James before he left Baltimore must still have reverberated in his mind. "I doubt whether I can endure the (metaphysical) climate of California for more than some two years. I shall grow consumptive (spiritually) and shall come East for my health. May the shade of good father Kant grant that I come not too late for recovery." Among these regrets in a letter to his old friend Gilman, he even confessed to missing the Gilman cat, "in her own playful little place." For many reasons Josiah found it hard to face California again. In his heart he already resolved, like Christian, "I must make a pilgrimage again someday."

CHAPTER 7

Berkeley Exile

Can you not understand what new vitality
I gain from this sojourn in desolate solitude?
Goethe, *Faust*

SARAH was fifty-nine years old when in late August 1878
her son, her beloved son, returned. She adored him, and he
had proved himself to his teacher-mother by studying abroad
and earning a Ph.D., the highest academic degree, one that at
the time honored only a handful of American scholars. What
joy to have him home bathed in accomplishment! Her other
children were gone. Mary Eleanor, after teaching in Marin
County, was now married, as was Harriette. Ruth was in San
Jose, where she had graduated the year before from the State
Normal School and accepted a job teaching in the preparatory
class. San Jose became Ruth's home base; in 1881 she became
the college's librarian and remained such until 1918.

Sarah's chief burden was her husband. The health of the
elder Royce, now sixty-six, had broken down; the family did
not expect him ever to work again, though he was gradually
recovering. The church was his refuge; he attended regular
services and weekly prayer meetings. He was a care, and the
strain of illness and declining income may have dictated their
frequent housing moves within the Oakland area. Of course,
nothing really changed; physical uprooting was Sarah's lot for
most of her life. The year her son left for Germany, the family
moved to 960 Clay Street in Oakland. That was the last time
the directories listed Josiah, Sr., the produce supplier or pro-
visioner. Thereafter the entries are under Mrs. S. E. Royce
alone. The year before Josie came back to Berkeley, her address
was San Pablo Street near Twenty-second. Not long after

came another change to Twenty-first Street between San Pablo
and Brush.

These last three moves in two years imply continuing unful-
fillment in the life of the elder Royces. The California immi-
grants' dream of settled plenty was no closer than ever. Prospects of old age and illness were disturbing. In these years, the
return of Josie was undoubtedly a bright upbeat for them. By
1880 Josiah lived with his parents (though the directory lists
only Josiah, Jr., and Mrs. Sarah E. Royce) at 523 Thirty-sixth
Street.

For Josie the move was far less uplifting. If the erudition
and the degree seemed like a pinnacle to his mother, for him
it was more like the first foothill, a faint beginning. He must
have hoped that something better would have come of his cre-
dentials, especially since he coveted, and nearly won, a Yale
position and some of his colleagues were kept at Johns Hopkins as assistant professors. The University of California was
not only out of the mainstream, it still did not even list a philosopher on its staff, let alone a department of philosophy.

For one who had sat in the shadow of monuments and ca-
thedrals, the cows grazing near the center of Oakland and the
little cluster of stores below the sparse Berkeley buildings were
at best a letdown, even to a romantic soul. Another personality
might have seen it differently. George Santayana was happy
that he had not been set down "where things supposed to be
important or exciting were happening, but in various quiet
places from which cross-vistas opened into the world." But,
then, he was describing Harvard, not the Far West, as the
out-of-the-way place. Royce felt more like a spider who had
climbed laboriously to the top of a tall building (in this case
an academic tower) and was now in danger of dying by starvation. At times "I would willingly throw everything over-
board and run away into a corner for the rest of my days."
Pilgrim was menaced by Despair in the Castle of Doubt. Certainly he saw few cross-vistas opening into the world from
Berkeley.

Bernard Moses, who in December 1875 arrived fresh from

Josiah's sisters: top left, Mary Eleanor Royce; right, Harriette (Hattie) Royce; lower left, Ruth Royce. (Courtesy of Nancy A. Hacker)

study in Germany to become the university's first professor of history, recalled "a row of cottages on the south side of the university grounds, designed for the use of professors and their families. There were ten or twelve houses scattered over the countryside, the beginning of the town."

In the subsequent three years the settlement grew toward Oakland, and the young instructor took up residence with his mother and father on Thirty-sixth Street, between Telegraph and Grove. The horse cars up Telegraph Avenue were supplemented now with steam dummies, mechanized vehicles that could pull a second, larger trolley in peak hours. In the fall of 1878 the Harmon Gymnasium was built, but not much else had changed since he left in 1875.

The college, suffering from anti-intellectual, populist feelings in the society at large, enrolled only 332 students (277 men, 55 women). Royce greeted familiar faculty faces. In the presidency Gilman had been replaced by John LeConte, who inherited the job without the skill. Joseph LeConte with bristling side-whiskers was in his prime, enthusiastically emphasizing his topics in geology and endorsing evolution. Paul Pioda and William Welcker still taught French and mathematics. One of Josie's classmates, William Carey Jones, was an instructor in Latin; and another, his chessmate Joseph C. Rowell, headed the library. Best of all, there was Edward Rowland Sill, with his tall frame and bright wit, the only professor of English and the chief reason for Royce's being there. They all experienced the kind of thinking illustrated by the regent who offered Bernard Moses his job.

> It is most desirable that all persons connected with it [the university] should have that tact, adaptation, and enthusiasm, that will enable them to take things as they *are*. . . . As the duties devolved upon different men in different departments, are not rigidly defined in all cases, a general lend-a-hand spirit, a cooperative ability, is most important.

Sill had written Gilman in the spring of 1878 for suggestions to fill the assistantship in English. In his few years at Berkeley, the poet-teacher had succeeded "in creating a demand for

English studies," though he lamented that "in practice the Mathematics still ride us like a nightmare." To help maintain the English momentum, he wanted a young man, receptive, with "a genuine love of literature and quickness to comprehend it," "a good mental philosopher," adept in Latin, Greek, and German. "He should be a good writer and speaker (both of these in the natural, i.e., modern style) and so the cause of it in others." And, finally he should be a man "with a bit of aesthetics about his brains somewhere." Sill hoped to get this paragon for $150 a month. Gilman's immediate nomination was Josiah Royce.

Not long after Sill welcomed Royce, he wrote Gilman, "Royce has been duly received, and found to answer the description." Sill worried about the German training, for he believed that only English education produced "thoroughly civilized men." Nevertheless, he catered to Royce's independence and let him teach logic in addition to his English courses.

In spite of their differences on the Germans, Sill and Royce continued to get along beautifully. They felt themselves apostles in the land of the philistines. Many of the regents, many of the faculty, and large numbers of the community, most especially the local editor Henry George, clamored for the practical in education, seeing specializations other than agriculture and the mechanic arts as domains of "kid-gloved professors," who acted like gods among the clouds on the Berkeley hills.

The library was one flinty point at issue. It now contained over fifteen thousand volumes, but that was not the problem. The books did not circulate and were little used by students or faculty. When Sill arrived, the library's doors were open for only one hour a day. Rowell had expanded the daily hours from one to eight, but the year Royce arrived the average daily users, students and faculty combined, were only thirty. Sill and Royce, hoping to get students into the library, assigned outside reading and insisted that classes use other than textbooks. Sill felt Royce his sole ally, "and I could hug him for it."

The new instructor taught five freshman and sophomore classes in English literature, composition, and rhetoric. In the spring of Royce's first year, Sill also let him teach logic to the freshmen and later to seniors. There were no other courses in philosophy. The young teacher fretted that he had to prepare this course too hastily, often the same day as the lecture. In retrospect he called it "dialectically a tolerable success and pedagogically a monstrous failure." The response to Royce from at least one student differed considerably. Young Harriet Lane from San Francisco missed him when he left and commented on his red hair and "his deep blue eyes [that] looked down into mine kindly, as if he liked me."

In one of his early lectures he compared philosophy to the domestic economy of a house; to understand it you do not look at a brick but at the kitchen: "And logic is the kitchen, the cookery room of Philosophy." His appreciation for logic was hereby affirmed, to be reinforced later when he came under the influence of Charles Sanders Peirce.

The course indirectly resulted in his first published book. It was "a logic textbook for one of my classes," and he started on it during his first summer vacation. But, as most young instructors have experienced in connection with their writing, other matters interferred. He had to prepare for his courses in English literature; he had promised to William Torrey Harris in St. Louis a book review on Shadworth Hodgson's *Philosophy of Reflection*; and his own speculations always soaked up his time. "Getting more and more puzzled about the ways of human thinking, I have extended my study to mathematics." So that summer he also worked with developments in geometry and quaternions as avenues into understanding Boole and Venn.

Meanwhile with the textbook, he was "snarled on the principles between Lotze [his professor in Germany] and some others." Nevertheless, in time the snarls unraveled, and the following year (1881) his *Primer of Logical Analysis for the Use of Composition Students* appeared. His book's intent was to inspire students to "reflect upon the meaning of speech." There is no denying his premise that good writing must be based on sound reasoning, but it is hard to imagine his freshmen students, especially those from the farms of Stockton or the mines of Grass Valley, appreciating his approach. He instructed them in the laws of logic using complex algebraic formulae and applying them to inference, terms, sentences, and grammar. For all its erudition, the text's examples reflect an author who has lived in the West, or at least in rural America. Grammatical assertions are about quail in the brush. Those who expect to understand language without study "might as well expect to become railway engineers merely by riding in railway carriages." "Nobody becomes a blacksmith by looking at a shod horse or at a wheel-tire."

He supplemented his meager income by helping edit a series of five graded school readers for the Bancroft Company in San Francisco. His colleagues on the project were prestigious educators, Charles H. Allen and John Swett. Allen, with flowing white beard and wire-rimmed glasses, headed the State Normal School at San Jose where Ruth Royce, his neighbor, counted herself practically a member of the Allen family. Josiah through his sister was also on friendly terms with Allen. Though a poet and friend of John Muir, Allen had come to education through the manual arts and must have buttressed Royce's sense of the practical, that miner's boy and engineer now buried within him. Swett shared with Royce a close relationship to a New England schoolteacher. State superintendent in the 1860s, he had been as important as the Easterners Horace Mann and Henry Barnard in demanding support and respect for the public schools.

The *New England Journal of Education*, comparing the Royce-Allen-Swett textbooks with McGuffey's readers, advertised: "Probably no three men in this country are better qualified, from practical experience and ability, to edit a series of school readers." For Royce that was real hyperbole. It is doubtful that his studies in Kantian Idealism, Boolean logic, and Sanskrit were necessary to compile snippets from Whittier, Longfellow, Shakespeare, Tennyson, and Byron for fifth graders. He knew the sources, of course, and perhaps that was enough. Twenty-two years later, with modesty and resignation, he denigrated his contribution "as having been of no great importance in the original enterprise. I did my little share of work; my coeditors were elder and wiser men. They largely overruled my opinions and were doubtless right in so doing."

During his first spring of teaching, he wrote Gilman that he was not much aware of university affairs, but what appears to be almost a boast may have reflected feelings of exclusion from membership in the academic senate. "I attend Faculty meetings but seldom, and seldom find myself lifted nearer heaven when I do." The following year, however, his rank brought him into the senate, and he became a dutiful attender, whether lifted heavenward or not. Of the eighty-six meetings between 1879 and 1882 for which the roll was taken, he was there 80 percent of the time, an extremely good record. He was not a prime mover, certainly not compared with the established figures such as LeConte, Kellogg, Welcker, Hilgard, and Sill, but he did act as recorder on one occasion, made several motions regarding students, and was involved with committees awarding medals for scholarship.

Far more rewarding to him than his teaching or his university service were the clubs he joined. Sill sponsored his election into the Berkeley Club, a collection of professors, clergy, lawyers, and businessmen who met in Oakland twice a month for dinner, papers, and talk. Gilman organized the group in his first year at the university. "We were lonesome in a crowd," he said, meaning the university in the midst of an intellectual community. Sill was a good example of the crowd, for while at the Oakland High School he was among the first nominated. In his own hand Royce later recorded the qualifications for a member.

A real education in the thorough and broad sense, so that he stands intelligently on his own base, and does his own thinking.

A genial nature and a social disposition, which can enjoy a meeting and can both make and take a joke.

Not so jaded that he can not command himself, not so engaged that he can not command his time, as a rule.

> That kind of benevolence which makes him a well-wisher of humanity, and glad to contribute to the wellfare [sic] of any select circle of active and thinking men.

Royce read four papers to the Berkeley Club (on pessimism, human thought, George Eliot, and evolution) and three more during subsequent trips to the San Francisco Bay area (on California history and primitive taboos). Serving as its secretary-treasurer for the 1879–80 year, the minutes reveal his dry humor.

> The secretary having been unable to deny that the Club's treasury was empty, an assessment of fifty cents was levied, and paid by those present.

> The adjournment took place at some late hour which the Secretary forgot to note.

> After this episode [an airing of San Francisco politics] and the bright visions of the great good the Club might do by discussing these practical problems had come for a time to an end, the members returned to thoughts about Celtic literature, and discussed that topic until 10 o'clock.

He made good friends here. He heard Bernard Moses talk on revolution and social growth; LeConte on evolution; Sill on Herbert Spencer; a retired lawyer turned historian, William W. Crane, on forces in American history.

There were other intellectual outlets, more strictly faculty groups. Bernard Moses held a Fortnightly Club for social scientists that Royce frequented and to which in the spring of 1880 he read a philosophical paper on human progress. It was published in the club's journal, the money for which had been given by William W. Crane of the Berkeley Club. In this article Royce turned his back on social Darwinism and proposed the improvement of society through reason, ideals, and will. He saw some point to the conservative who "lops the mouldering branch away" and thereby changed "old conditions to meet new needs, in such a way as shall involve the least possible expenditure of energy," but he sympathized more with what he called the optimist. This is not the person as in a western mining camp who is solely geared to future success, rather the one who acts with self-sacrifice, with "a faith that individual efforts, if lost for the individual himself, are not lost for his community, that the combined effect of everybody's efforts is progress and general good." Change may thus be guided by a search for unity and "the courage that can face possible, even probable destruction, with the delight of a hero." An expansion of these ideas underscored Royce's later writings on the history of California.

Articles of this period reveal similar themes. The world is essentially social, not individual. A life that is devoted to individual ends must result in pessimism. "Do not make men unhappy by telling them that were they a little more wealthy or politically a little freer, they would be happy. Tell them that they can find happiness only when they cease to seek it for themselves. Talk no more of golden ages. Talk of golden deeds."

One of the papers he read to the Psychology Club (which he helped Sill organize) commemorated the death of Ralph Waldo Emerson in Concord. Emerson was for him a kindred thinker, a rejecter of utilitarian ethics, a believer in the spirit that transcended materialism, and a devoted lover of the organic unity that is nature. Still Royce was not a simple follower of Emerson. "Not that I am a disciple myself. The condition whose presence saves [one] from Pessimism, is unfortunately lacking in my case; and though I am not properly a Pessimist, I am a dabbler in dangerous problems, and a very extensive doubter."

In Berkeley Royce kept a "Thought Diary." From these notes on his reading, on intellectual problems, and on plans for future work emerge other clues to the energy and breadth of his mind. In them was much philosophy, of course (Kant and Hegel and Peirce), but there was also a variety of literature—Rousseau (*Nouvelle Héloïse*), Morley on Rousseau and the sublimity of nature, and, predictably, Goethe with ruminations on *Manfred* and *Faust* ("The essence of life and being is activity"). Goethe was still for him the crown of modern poetry.

In the same diary on February 12, 1879, he headed a page "Meditations before the Gate" and revealed himself and his situation as in few other places.

> I am a Californian; and day after day, by the order of the World Spirit (whose commands we all do ever obey, whether we will it or no) I am accustomed to be found at my tasks in a certain place that looks down upon the Bay of San Francisco and over the same out into the waters of the western Ocean. . . . Here as I do my work I often find time for contemplation.

There follows a rapturous passage on the beauties of the bay, the sea, and the sky.

> The long lines of fog, born in through the Gate or through the depressions of the range, stretch out over many miles of country like columns of an invading host, now shining in innocent whiteness as if their mission were but one of love, now becoming dark and dreadful, as when they smother the sun at evening. So, while the year goes by, one is never without the companionship of Nature. And there are heroic deeds done in cloud-land, if one will but look forth and see them.

Then, after some attention to stricter questions of philosophy:

> With these problems I shall seek to busy myself earnestly, because that is each one's duty; independently, because I am a Californian, as little bound to follow mere tradition as I am liable to find an audience by preaching in this wilderness; reverently, because I am thinking and writing face to face with a mighty and lovely Nature, by the side of whose greatness I am but as a worm.

Royce, the misplaced young man, was torn between a ravishing western setting in which he should be completely happy ("could a truly noble soul be nourished by the continual sight of the nature that is here, [such a] soul would be not a little enviable") and his independent desire ("because I am a Californian") to flee the wilderness that provided his thinking with no responsive audience.

The struggle was not unlike the human predicament, and the counsel of a later and wiser Royce was to find in the battle itself the answer to the problem of evil. But in the year he wrote his "Meditations before the Gate" a woman was entering his life in the fullest sense, and she made his last sustained period in the West worth the trial and the predicament.

Katharine Head claimed that she first saw Josiah Royce in the fall of 1878 when he rushed across the main reading room of the library to greet his old classmate and chessmate Joseph Rowell. Katharine was an undergraduate at the time, and the meeting must have been noisy to have drawn her attention and remained in her memory. Either that or she was instinctively attracted to Josiah.

It is probable that they met formally through Edward Sill, for the Head family, prominent in Oakland, was well acquainted with Sill. Katharine's father, Edward Francis Head, a Bostonian and graduate of Harvard, was a wealthy, respected superior court judge of San Mateo County. He lost his sight after taking the bench and became known as the blind judge. Her sister, Anna, founded a preparatory school for girls in Berkeley that was destined for a prestigious history. Katharine herself was schooled at Miss Hubbard's in Boston, studying Latin, French, and German. She was short, with bright blue eyes and a long, aristocratic nose. Truly talented, she translated literature, published stories and poems, played Chopin brilliantly, and would undoubtedly have gone further with her music except for her tiny hands, which could not span an octave.

Details of the courtship of Josiah and Katharine are shrouded in restraint. There were undoubtedly dinners at the Head house, genteel and sparkling, especially when they included Edward Sill. There must have been walks in the Berkeley hills; Josiah loved that scene too much not to share it. We wonder if he read to her from his favorite poets—Shelley, Tennyson, Browning—his red hair and round white forehead like a gnome in the shadows of the trees. Over twenty years later on a trip to Berkeley, he happily showed his son "the lovers'

Josiah and Katharine. Probably in their early Cambridge years. The two had a warm but not demonstrative relationship. (Courtesy of Nancy A. Hacker)

walk." If it was so important in his mind, might he and Katharine not have strolled there as young lovers? By January 1880 Josiah and Katharine were engaged to be married, and a laconic Royce wrote James, "Socially I am well off."

In happy succession, his parents decided to move to Los Gatos, perhaps to be nearer Ruth, and the Heads transferred to Redwood City, offering Josiah and Katharine their house in Berkeley. The two were married—he twenty-four, she twenty-two—in Berkeley on October 2, 1880. They must have lived with or near the Heads for a time because young Royce ran the dogs each morning and evening.

A measure of contentment, not complete, but clearly present, crept into his letters. The following January he wrote Charles Lanman, "My contemplative existence I pursue over tea in the evenings, or on afternoon walks on the hills that look westward out of the Golden Gate into the sea." His friend answered, "I can hardly think of you as married, you with boyish look and fresh heart." Come back to Cambridge, he suggested, check my beliefs while I teach you the Bhagavad Gita, and "I would let you roll my dumb-bells all over the floor and give you caramels ad lib." Whatever Royce thought about Lanman's offer, he was comporting successfully with his father-in-law. Judge Head, already with one blind eye, wrote the following spring that Kitty and Royce "get along admirably. He is a splendid little fellow and the O. L. [old lady?] and I are almost as fond of him as K[itty]."

The marriage of Josiah and Katharine held real advantage for the young philosopher. Through it he gained a social standing that he had known before only peripherally through Gilman's letters of introduction or the friendship of people like Sill. And with the status also came resources, for hereafter on crucial occasions in both Berkeley and later in Cambridge, his wife's family provided the children with comfortable housing that they could otherwise ill afford. But there was, of course, more. Josiah and Katharine shared common intellectual interests in literature and music. And focusing it all was affection, not always overt and sometimes troubled, but never lacking. In April 1882 Katharine bore their first son, Christopher. He was a great joy and later a great sorrow in their marriage and, like their other children, a strong cement. Their offspring added immeasurably to the respect the parents held for one another. The tenderness between Josiah and Katharine was matched and exceeded by devotion for their boys.

In the spring of 1882 the young father anticipated the appearance of three of his philosophical articles—one on mind, one on Kant, and one on beliefs (in which he used the phrase "the will to believe," later picked up by James). These articles attracted philosophical attention and showed that, in fact, California proved a rather fertile environment for him. Yet he continued to feel isolated, particularly bereft of criticism. To James he confided about one of his theories, "In this wilderness with nobody to talk with about it, I have not the least idea whether it is true or not." Matters worsened when Sill decided to leave Berkeley. The poet concluded, as he said later, that California was "one part fever and two parts sham." There was some prospect that Sill's post would be offered Royce, but Royce feared such an appointment "as a snare of the devil to tempt me from my real business." He continued to write Gilman and Coale of his "great desire to find a position nearer to civilization."

When William James wrote with the prospect of replacing him at Harvard for a year, the sun broke through. It was a temporary position at $1,250 a year, the remainder of James's half-pay sabbatical salary. Tempted at the same time with the remote possibility of staying at Berkeley, Royce knew that Harvard was a gamble. The young man, however, surveyed California and concluded, "I should regard an egg in Cambridge as worth more than a brood of chickens here." "I am very ready to go," he wrote James, "and eager to accept your offer."

James thought he would be well advised to come alone, leaving Katharine and the baby Christopher with her parents for the school year. But Royce was confident, anxious to risk all, too intoxicated about the prospects to plan for a return. His father, after all, had not left his mother and little Mary Eleanor in Iowa in 1849. Christopher, three weeks old, was younger than Mary Eleanor had been, but Royce wrote, "I shall be overjoyed at the thought of bringing him up in an Eastern atmosphere." To Gilman he described excitedly his "chance, for a time at least, to live in a studious community and to do my own work. What becomes of me and my family after the end of a year does not appear, but I am very willing to take risks in a good cause." Gilman responded that the move was "venturesome" but "an earnest of future success."

Bunyan's Christian now walked with Hopeful having found the Key called Promise. Royce's resignation to the president and the regents of the University of California was unprovisional, to take place on September 1, 1882, with no requests for leave, no apologies, no appreciations, no regrets. He was far more emotional to his Baltimore friend, Charles Lanman, his guru of Sanskrit and the Bhagavad Gita, who now held a regular position in Cambridge. "I go to Harvard with a mixture of trembling and impudence that will doubtless be charming to witness when I arrive. Doubtless I shall blunder through a year in some fashion, and I shall hope at all events to make no enemies, unless it be by my ugly face and my Californian barbarity."

"So it is now set down," he wrote without sadness, and the die that was cast marked the end of Royce's years in California. He returned only for short visits to family and friends. On two occasions he spent a whole summer there. But the formative time was finished. Though he always called himself a Californian, the setting for the Westerner was henceforth on a different stage. If he projected the West, even subtly through his written and spoken words, he now had a wider audience, the kind the West so frequently sought. It would indirectly include the admirers of Cooper and Bierstadt and Wister, and more directly a rarefied group of intellectuals largely unaware of the sources of their inspiration.

CHAPTER 8

Harvard

The way of reflection is long. The forest of our common human ignorance is dark and tangled. Happy indeed are those who are content to live and to work only in regions where the practical labors of civilization have cleared the land, and where the task of life is to till the fertile fields and to walk in the established ways.

Royce, *The World and the Individual*

I go gather this
The sacred knowledge, here and there dispersed
About the world, long lost or never found.

Browning, *Paracelsus*

CHARLES Rieber—philosopher, dean, onetime student of Royce in Cambridge—told his children, "All that will be remembered about Harvard 400 years from now will be that Josiah Royce once taught there." No such paeans could have been predicted when the twenty-six year old Royce arrived after eleven days crossing the continent with a wife and newborn son to fill a temporary position.

For the first two years Royce taught at Harvard on uncertain tenure, as substitute for James and then as a replacement for another good friend, George Herbert Palmer. The third year was only a slight improvement: an instructorship with the promise of an assistant professorship on the next vacancy. In the fall of 1885 he secured his first regular appointment. He remained at Harvard for the rest of his life. The gamble had paid off. And the West now became a place to visit his parents and sisters, a patchwork of memories, mostly unshared with his new society.

On arrival the Royces rented a few rooms on Sumner Street, not far from the Yard. Here they lived until his position was regularized, and in 1885 they moved to 20 Lowell Street in a pleasant neighborhood close to the Charles River. Christopher was then growing up, "a jolly fat boy," somewhat precocious, who enjoyed listening to his mother at the piano more than playing with other boys. Who could then imagine his eventual tragedy? For a time Mary's daughter, Eleanor, lived with them while she attended high school. In their earliest Cambridge years, they felt themselves social outcasts, but in time they invited friends over for musical evenings and were often enough sought by hostesses who valued Royce's conversational gambits. His sensitivity at being looked down on for his western manners was transmuted into something approaching pride in his background.

For years, however, he felt his western past as an encumbrance, even a barrier in old-line New England. The Brahmin William James was a staunch and loving friend, but Royce could hardly have been unaware that James's wife, Alice, disliked him. Once in 1889 she must have told him so, for he soothed James's consequent embarrassment with a note: "I haven't been an odious little creature all these years without fully knowing the fact, and I think of none so highly as I do of those who share my appreciation of the odiousness in question." Possibly more than philosophical views lay behind his comment in 1908 that "the 'Pragmatists' wag their heads and mock when I pass by." As late as 1912 he confided to a friend, "I never was, in my youth, a person 'cultivated' in any aesthetic sense; and I remain more barbarous as to such matters than you can easily suspect." Royce was the ugly duckling, and his background in his early Harvard years was only minimally acceptable.

But he never denied his California roughness, never tried to hide it, and even defied the conventions, as when he continued to wear his battered western straw hat. To paraphrase the son of the middle border, Hamlin Garland, who at the same time was adjusting to Boston, he "remained immutably" of the West. He was not a rebel; neither was he submissive. If he wished contacts with Westerners, as the years went by, there were opportunities. Californians came to study at Harvard, and at one time in 1896 when Joseph LeConte visited Royce, the naturalist was pleased to find a Berkeley colony that numbered over twenty.

The Harvard of Josiah Royce was the Harvard of President Charles W. Eliot, who, by attracting scholars in professional schools and graduate study, was in the process of catalyzing America's oldest college into a truly distinguished institution. Specialization in academic disciplines was slowly emerging, as it was at Johns Hopkins. At Harvard it was happening in history with Edward Channing, in English with George Lyman Kittredge, and likewise in economics and geology and chemistry. It was about to follow in philosophy; when James was joined by Royce and George Herbert Palmer and they in turn elevated George Santayana and Hugo Münsterberg, academic philosophy was being born, not only at Harvard, but in America.

Royce with his omniverous intellect must have been equally impressed with the new world that daily unfolded around him—Henry Van Dyke and Lyman Abbott preaching in the chapel, James Bryce and Carrie Nation and William Osler lecturing, Henry Irving and Otis Skinner and Maude Adams playing in the Boston theaters.

Now in the classroom Josiah touched and influenced, not the farm boys of Fresno or the rough products of San Francisco, but a rare cluster of the minds of turn-of-the-century America: George Santayana, C. I. Lewis, George Herbert Mead, William Ernest Hocking, Helen Keller, Horace Kallen, W. E. B. DuBois, Randolph Bourne, Ludwig Lewisohn, A. O. Lovejoy, T. S. Eliot, Oliver Wendell Holmes, Woodrow Wilson, Franklin D. Roosevelt. For all their praise of him, these men never created around Royce a school. He had no use for the teacher who makes "mere disciples." No missionary, he sought no converts. One of his doctoral oral students thought to improve his chances by parroting the ideas of his mentor. Royce was displeased and threatened the student with an R.D. (Doctor of Royce) instead of a Ph.D.

Royce liked teaching. John Jay Chapman, his student, versified his teacher's words.

> A joy it is to learn, I know,
> A joy in all men's reach,
> And therefore little prized; but, oh,
> The joy it is to teach!

Like most good teachers, he preferred the one-on-one, or the small seminar. Royce considered lecturing to be a form of vanity, especially "when addressed to the passively receptive mind." It did not allow the hearer to meditate or the speaker to be either concise or exhaustive. Actually his lectures seldom reached the average undergraduate, who rarely understood him, though the student "always had a sense that something big was going on." Still, whatever the level, Royce never discouraged an earnest mind. To one entering undergraduate he seemed "human and humorous and kind." He looked charitably on "painstaking work, even if mediocre," finding in average papers "insights and motives of which their authors were blissfully unconscious." On papers from his undergraduate courses, he wrote pages of comments; sometimes he scrawled over his own lines in two directions, even if the paper was assigned only a grade of B. To a page of remarks on one twelve-page B-paper, he added, "Your tendency is to be over brief."

In the graduate seminar he achieved his true effectiveness. Around the table with a select few, he invited opposition, delighting in thrusts aimed at his own arguments. Richard Cabot once fearfully presented Royce with a paper that he felt was devastating to Royce's thought, full of "heavy metal." Royce was more pleased with it than anything Cabot ever did. To the seminar Royce invited visiting thinkers from all departments. There would follow "an amicable altercation between Royce and his guests." On one such occasion the notes of a student, Victor Lenzen, seemed to be reporting a tennis game with the arguments of the proponents flying first to Royce's court, then to the other. This respect for the ideas of others was not a far cry from his mother's simpler teaching; he was raised, after all, in an environment where books and ideas were precious and prized.

The Royce who left the Berkeley hills for the Harvard Yard still was notable for his bright red hair, not yet muted into the later distinguished cloud of white. That unusual glare of red intensified Royce's self-reliant appearance, like Hugh Walpole's character Crispin, whose red hair sprung up like a challenge, "something alive of its own independence." Royce lived in a day when drawing psychological conclusions from physiognomy, like the cranial bumps of phrenology, was serious and popular. When he was seven, old enough to have read it, the Grass Valley newspaper carried such a piece on red hair. "A red head is always accompanied with a delicately fair skin and light eyes; these indicate . . . the nervous or intellectual nature, forming when properly regulated, one of the finest organizations in the world; very generous, very affectionate, 'go-ahead-ative' and intelligent."

It was not a bad description of Josiah. Beneath his hair was indeed a pink, florid, freckled complexion, bushy red eyebrows, golden eyelids, and blue eyes ("the bluest, and the most quizzically kindly, that could be imagined," said his son). And his giant forehead suggested, if not proved, intelligence. His hat size was $7 \frac{5}{8}$. That head was compared once with a young Ben Franklin and, more often, with Ludwig van Beethoven; his eyes indeed held some of the twinkle of Franklin; and his outsized cranium, the impressiveness of Beethoven. He was jokingly aware that others likened his visage to a combined cherub and toad. His stature contributed to that more diminished impression; he was five and a half feet tall and a bit round. But he was stockily strong with heavy chest and shoulders.

His handwriting suggested the incongruity of the exterior. Large, craggy letters rambled in lines across the page. Lanman joshed his friend on "those singularly unangular characters

Josiah, 1885. Royce in the mid-1880s, probably not long after he moved from California to Harvard. (Courtesy of the Harvard University Archives)

which go chasing each other down hill in so friendly fashion."
Perhaps the repression of his innate left-handedness caused the
wandering immaturity of his penmanship. Susan Sontag once
described the handwriting of the refugee radical Walter Benjamin as microscopic, miniaturized to make it more portable,
appropriate for a wanderer and refugee who wished to con-
ceal. If she analyzed Royce, she might conversely read into his
colossal writing a personality geared to permanence, open
availability, revelation, even a large cooperative world.

The same expansivenesss was reflected in food and drink.
William James and George Herbert Mead, friends who should
have known, feared that Royce's "foolish eating and drinking"
habits led to a neglect of his health. He smoked so much that
a newspaper reporter noted the fact in 1891, and an extant to-
bacconist's bill indicates that in 1905 he bought two hundred
cigars on June 6 and another two hundred on July 11.

The most charitable descriptions said that he dressed plainly.
There were accounts of his thin overcoats, his unconventional
clothes, his rumpled trousers, his forgetfulness in putting on a
tie for morning chapel (compulsory chapel was not abolished
until 1886). His old western hat, of which he seemed so proud,
topped an apparel that led one student to think "his 'get-up'
in general was not fashionable. The whole had the uncouth air
that made its own appeal: he was handsome from very plain-
ness," an "original in looks."

Not many listeners, though, were allowed time to analyze
his appearance, for his conversation too quickly rose like a
wave to engulf them. One undergraduate compared his dic-
tion to "the continuous flow of a river." He became known in
the Yard as one whose answer to a question might take an
hour. John Jay Chapman remembered their first meeting, sitting by chance across from Royce at Park's Oyster House after
a concert in Boston.

> He began to talk to me about Beethoven, and he was talking
> exactly as if he had known me all my life. Royce was the only
> human being I have ever seen who had no preliminary social
> consciousness, no door-mat of convention. You were inside,

though you didn't know how you got there. . . . [He] was a bumblebee—a benevolent monster of pure intelligence, zig-zagging, ranging, and uncatchable. I always had this feeling about Royce—that he was a celestial insect. If left alone with him, any one would be apt to turn into a naturalist through the effort to catalogue him.

His conversation amazed people, full of "jests, humor, and astounding analogies drawn from passing events and from current fiction." Some of the torrent came from his desire to qualify, to dissect. He must have been what John Muir was to his father: "a contumacious quibbler too fond of disputation." But with Royce it was not debate for debate's sake. He once wrote: "It is as fickle to disagree with everybody as to agree with everybody. And the man who always opposes is as much the slave of external fortune as the man who always agrees." William Ernest Hocking described Royce's conversation as "enlarging and lifting the horizon of whatever subject he touched, in whose presence invisible things took on substance and our petty selves dropped away." And it all came through in a voice that was variously thin, voluble, strident, or "as soft and delicate" as that of Desdemona. Horace Kallen said Royce's speech "seemed often a private soliloquy publicly continued as he was entering his class-room and taking off his coat." Two future presidents of the United States felt the spell of that voice, Woodrow Wilson and Franklin Roosevelt; it was Wilson who recorded the fullest effect. "The dullest fellow at the board listened with delight . . . because he has the faculty of bringing masses of detail into a single luminous picture where they are grouped with a perfection of perspective and a skill of harmonious arrangement which fill the novice, the would-be historical painter, with despair."

That "single luminous picture" succinctly described Royce's thought processes. He increasingly saw wholeness in particulars. He delighted in elevating the commonplace; he would quote from a streetcar transfer and illuminate the transit to eternity. Trivial incidents in life, like tips and gratuities, were fraught with universal import. More and more through his years the significance lay in oneness. "Have a plan; give unity to your aims," he would write. "I want to know the way that leads our human practical life homewards."

Royce held organized religion in high respect, but his Grass Valley rebellion from church attendance never relaxed. The extreme of his parents' zealous commitment along with his own independence ("because I am a Californian") provoked a life-long reluctance to find the inner religious experience of primary concern. His emancipation from fundamentalism was only deepened by the intellectual buffetings of Berkeley in the 1870s. He remembered how serious can be those times when we "revise some trustfully accepted creed of childhood. The foundations of the great deep are broken up. The old life of simple faith lies behind us. We can no longer rest there. We look out into the darkness of a world that is not now brightened by happy confidence." As an adult he felt that the church posed a danger in which the particulars might be confused with the divine. He feared that unreflective feelings, "mere visceral sensations" on Sunday morning or at prayer, might become the goal of religion. Royce never was a churchgoer, though ironically, his elder son, Christopher, was confirmed in Christ Church (Episcopal) in Cambridge, and Edward sang in the church choir.

Royce was, nevertheless, a thoroughly religious man. He spent most of his professional life in searching out the proper relations between religion and philosophy. He felt no more inconsistency between the two than LeConte observed between religion and science. A primary role of philosophy, Royce believed, was to test the truth of religion. In the years ahead, as his friendship with William James deepened, he joked that James was only testing how religion can be useful, while he, Royce, was asking whether it was true.

The first book Royce published after his arrival at Harvard, based on lectures he gave that first year, *The Religious Aspect of Philosophy: A Critique of the Bases of Conduct and of Faith* (1885), was a landmark in his religious inquiries. "The religious problems," he wrote, "have been chosen for the present study because they first drove the author to philosophy, and because they, of all human interests, deserve our best efforts and our utmost loyalty." In this work Royce proved the presence of an Absolute through the existence of error. Error was a mere "torso, a piece of driftwood, neither true nor false." It would not be possible without an Absolute, because lacking a third element, there is no way of proving the rightness or wrongness of any event. "All truth is truth because it is known by a conscious Thought." (If wishing to reconstruct this abstruse argument, the reader should see John E. Smith's article in *Meaning, Truth, and God*, ed. Leroy S. Rouner.) Frank Oppenheim has called Royce's work the first of three milestones in the overall development of his final philosophy, because here he unequivocally left his early skepticism and accepted the idea of the Absolute. In social terms, "We thus must see ourselves as little members of a vast body, as little fragments of a mighty temple, as single workers whose work has importance only by reason of its relations to the whole." And if this doctrine is accepted, "whatever becomes of the old creeds in the present religious crisis, the foundations of genuinely religious faith are sure."

His most mature religious insights came in *The Problem of Christianity* (1913), probably his finest book in style and thought. Faced with the dilemmas posed by science to religion (evolution vs. creation, for example), modern Christians tend to reduce their faith to a moral-ethical code; retreat to the teachings and parables of Jesus alone; ignore later accretions such as the Trinity, predestination, atonement, and grace; trivialize Christianity by reducing it to Jesus appearing in a Chicago settlement house. For Royce these approaches were woefully incomplete. To the moral code and Christ's life must be added the fuller understanding of the Kingdom of God, which came through Paul and his message on the Christian community, what Royce called the Beloved Community. The church, not the person of its founder, was the central idea of Christianity. The community was the final instrument of salvation. Royce thus turned from the religious modernists of his day and circled back to embrace, though reinterpret, some of the oldest verities of Christianity. A latter-day Puritan braided the strands of the sacred and the profane.

Whatever his work in religion, Royce's task was that of all philosophers, "a patient wandering in the wilderness of ignorance until he sees the road home." Home was a total philosophical system. He was not content until he had systematically covered metaphysics, epistemology, logic, and ethics. Charles Sanders Pierce, no mean systematizer himself, compared Royce in this respect with his fellows.

> As for the whole existing race of philosophers,—say John Dewey, to mention a relatively superior man whom you see,— why they are the sort of trash who are puzzled by Achilles and the Tortoise! Think of trying to drive any exact thought through such skulls! Royce is the only philosopher I know of real power of thought now living.

Unlike philosophy, politics in the sense of politicians and parties did not much interest Royce. Disinclined, even in the midst of California's hot debate over a new constitution in the 1870s, he missed his first opportunity to vote, "unable to warm with any patriotic fire in these days of political masquerade." He was fully aware of, yet not attracted to, the radicalism of his time. Once in a lecture he claimed to be an idealistic socialist, and in his writings threw side-glances at Henry George and the Populists (though not at Karl Marx). Royce never came close to embracing socialism. At best he found it "shadowy" and "mildly dangerous." At worst it was a wedge to split the community in twain. He was more concerned with theoretical political problems. As a child of the Progressive Era, he puzzled over the ambiguities of progress, and as with so many thinkers of the day—James, Santayana, Dewey, Peirce, and Henry Adams—he found the modern world spiritually wanting. It was an age of schism "when every new enlargement of our vast corporations is followed by a new development of strikes and of industrial conflicts." As in western mines and railroads, the misdeeds and unwise management of corporations compounded the vastness of corporate power.

One part of Royce worried about bigness and the impersonalization of urban life. He shared this concern with the Progressives and with the other golden-age philosophers. As James wrote, "The bigger the unit you deal with, the hollower, the more brutal, the more mendacious is the life displayed." When Royce spoke of "leveling tendencies" in America, he meant these same "vast forces that work toward industrial consolidation, and toward the effacement of individual initiative." But bigness was not in itself an evil, unless it was centralization unattended by the countervailing force of the provincial community and its attendant loyalties. It was less a question of size than the quality of attachment in a hierarchy of values. Royce accepted, even welcomed, the corporate growth of the American university—under Gilman at Johns Hopkins, Eliot at Harvard, Benjamin Ide Wheeler at Berkeley. But he saw such growth balanced by loyal subgroups, like fraternities for students and professional societies for faculty.

At the lower end of the social scale, modern workers faced the "dreary complexity of mechanical labor" and failed to find in their work any significance to the whole. "In fact, it is the original sin of any highly developed civilization that it breeds cooperation at the expense of a loss of interest in the community."

The vastness of corporate enterprise and the anomie of individual workers were fertile grounds for the extremes of individualism and collectivism, each intensifying and inflaming the other. "The more the social will expresses itself in vast organizations of collective power, the more are individuals trained to be aware of their own personal wants and choices and ideals, and of the vast opportunities that would be theirs if they could but gain control of these social forces." Thus it is that "the social order . . . trains the individual to be as great a sinner as his powers permit" and creates in the society "the original sin of social contentiousness."

Reform of the social structure might seem a consequential approach, but Royce held little confidence in the reformer, especially the radical or anarchist. He admitted that, in politics as in philosophy, the "extremes easily meet." Nevertheless, "as an agitator, the typically restless child of our age often insists upon heaping up new burdens of social control,—control that he indeed intends to have others feel rather than himself." Here Royce deviated from most Progressives of the Teddy Roosevelt–Hiram Johnson type; he was suspicious of reform through laws and bureaucratic regulations. If reform was merely a disparate collection of interest groups, as some recent historians have described progressivism, then reform was not for Royce. Old-line, pre-Progressive politics was a better source of overarching loyalties. This was indeed a Burkean brand of progressivism and had, to use the phrase of historian T. Jackson Lears, an antimodern flavor. "Physical science and the industrial arts are altering the very foundations of our culture, of our social order, and of our opinions regarding nature. This alteration is now taking place at a rate for which no previous age of human history furnishes any parallel."

In Royce's work there are unhappy metaphors of strangers and jostling crowds, a distaste for automobiles, commerce, committees, and class conflict, which reflect an aristocratic abhorrence of the new, but which might also suggest a populist or rural distrust of the city. But when Royce employs the city as a metaphor, it emerges as a vision of the eternal, the apocalyptic New Jerusalem, the Augustinian City of God. "Here upon earth we have no abiding city." However, "we all need the superhuman, the city out of sight, the union with all life,—the essentially eternal." That city out of sight is "the homeland where, perchance, we learn to understand one another."

The city stood in eternal opposition to the wilderness. Alone, isolated, filled with doubt, individuals in the wilderness use their isolation to understand and criticize but must return to the city in order to affirm. If they stay in the wilderness, they become self-serving hedonists, Leatherstockings in an agrarian utopia. If they remain in the city, they succumb to herd instincts. Royce came to see at Harvard that the wilderness and the city were not in opposition but should be com-

plementary and ceaselessly interacting. His romantic appreciation of nature coupled with his personal experience in an
embryonic western society provided him with a vision of
larger patriotic national commitments supported by smaller
face-to-face attachments. Thus Royce was a positive, even op-
timistic antimodern.

For the progressives there was a certain inevitability of progress. They knew what was necessary, they knew what made
people tick, and as professionals they could and would improve the world. Even for Marxists, capitalism would inevitably collapse of its own internal inconsistencies. But Royce
leaned too heavily on the power of the human will to partake
of any determinism. Will for Royce might lead beyond the
temporal and be subsumed in the Absolute, but that did not
undermine its significance in the present. Royce could thus be
compared only with those progressives such as Woodrow Wilson, Jane Addams, or Lincoln Steffens (in his social-gospel
period) who claimed morality as the base for their reforms.
His was the ethic of an Absolute defined in the spirit of the
genuine community.

Royce's interest and importance will always lie in his ideas,
but this fact should not blind us to his humanity. In his rise to
philosophical fame, he never lost sight of his family. He genuinely loved his wife, though neighbors and local gossipers created of her a shrew, a woman intent on derogatory comments
about Royce and his philosophy to guests at parties. But, if
true, these prove little about the fundamental relationship of
the two. Katharine was a remarkable woman, not only talented with piano and pen, but strong and stable. Her letters
to Josiah do not suggest an effusive love. He wrote to her with
phrases such as "I tell the dear sea-birds daily about them [the
children], as I have so often done in earlier voyages. And the
birds have messages for you, too." No such endearments appear in her letters to him, though she occasionally signed herself, "Yours with fondest love, Katharine Royce." By 1891 they
slept in separate bedrooms, but that was probably not un-

Josiah Royce. At the Daniel Coit Gilman home in Meadville, Pennsylvania, in 1902. That summer he also visited Berkeley, lecturing to the University of California summer session. The photograph denotes a mature self-possession along with a quizzical independence. (Courtesy of the Harvard University Archives)

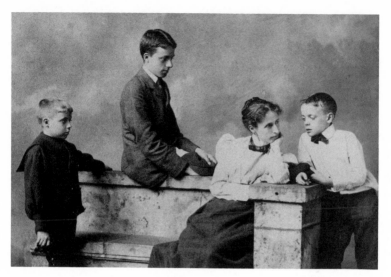

Katharine and the Royce sons. The boys, from left to right, are Stephen, Christopher, and Edward. (Courtesy of the Harvard University Archives)

usual in their time and place, and Royce's asthma could alone explain the arrrangement. When on a ship once, Royce was caught in a storm, the news made Katharine desperately miserable, and when the vessel was finally sighted, she wrote in her diary: "That is event enough for once. I shall probably not know or notice anything else." She was a help to Royce in his work; she was a ballast for his temperament, and he knew it.

They were both devoted to their three boys, Christopher, Edward, and Stephen, born three to four years apart between 1882 and 1889. It was a warm family. The boys called their mother Fuffy or Kitty or Mummum; she lovingly played them music. Royce was Papa or Popps; he took them on boating trips out of Martha's Vineyard or told them stories of days at sea or of California life in the mining camps. One of his favorites quoted a wooden headstone, "He done his damndest; angels could do no more."

Christopher, their special firstborn joy, whom they called

Coco, brought them their deepest sorrow. In childhood he suffered a spell of partial amnesia, unable to open his eyes, with constant movement of limbs and fingers. As a young man he experienced difficulty with jobs, unsuccessfully trying real estate and the financial world of New York, while always hoping to be a teacher like his father. By 1906 his parents grew concerned over his mental stability, and the next year he was brought home, suffering delusions, eventually needing restraint. Following a difficult and enormously expensive period, just after Christmas in the new year of 1908 he was committed to Danvers State Hospital, no longer controllable at home. Royce wrote William James that his pain was so great, he could not discuss it. James responded by giving money for a trust so that the boy need never become a helpless pauper. Contracting typhoid fever, Christopher died in 1910, the same year as James himself.

Edward (they called him Ned) was the most musical of the family. In his freshman year he received a D in history, but an A in music. Royce traveled at various times with Ned, once to New York and later to Bayreuth, where they heard "The Ring" together. The father wished for the son "that the world is as full of beauty to you as your dear good heart can find it." And apparently Ned uncovered much of that beauty in his career, studying music in Berlin, teaching at the Eastman School of Music, composing sonatas and a symphony, and eventually conducting the Ithaca Symphony Orchestra. He had, however, two disastrous marriages, and his retarded child, Randolph, rejected by his first wife, was left in the care of Katharine and Josiah.

The youngest boy, Stephen (Tephen to the family), suffered from asthma as badly as his father. Josiah once shepherded Stephen for months through California in an effort to abate that curse. Katharine reported that Stephen and his father, returning from an earlier trip, were "fonder of each other than ever." In spite of his affliction Stephen had a successful profession in engineering, but Josiah and Katharine, who had grown

to love Stephen's child, had to live through the sudden, shock-
ing death of the baby in 1915.

Royce seemed especially close to Stephen. The warmth
comes through in one particularly moving letter, written to
the young man on his first job in Colorado, where he wrestled
with filth, smells, and disappointments. "I need not say what
loving sympathy it arouses, nor yet need I tell how heartily
our dear Kitty joins with you in your sense of how intolerable,
for the time, the situation that you describe is." The father
then compared his son to a soldier in war. "Yet war they call
glorious. The only reason why war can be glorious is the mo-
tive of devotion, the honorable willingness to serve and to
stick, which makes even the nastiness something else than sick-
ening." He confessed that older men, as he himself had done,
use and watch and test younger men before they favor or ad-
vance them. Then a warm conclusion:

> Well, it rains, and Ned leaves us this evening, and the nights
> are often lonesome now, and the shadows are sometimes pretty
> deep. But we love Stephen, and his voice when it comes back
> to us, as it will, is one of the sweetest things that we ever hear.
> So keep our precious one for us, and it isn't long, after all,
> before home and you will be together again. Lovingly, Josiah.

As he matured, Josiah continued to enjoy music. A philosopher, he said, meaning to be complimentary, was "the professional musician of reflective thought." His mother's melodeon
lay deep in his memory, as did her romantic ability to trans-
port herself from a rude frontier cabin to a soaring cathedral
through the power of harmony. In letters to her, Josiah described concerts in Boston, and she once answered, "Those
delightful musical feasts—I can hardly forbear longing to enjoy them with you." Royce and Katharine communicated that
artistic sensibility to their sons, two of whom, Christopher
and Edward, became polished musicians.

The romantic composers, especially Beethoven, were Royce's
favorites. In the many references to music in his major philosophical works (usually in discussions of unity), Beethoven is

mentioned most often, followed by Wagner and Schubert. Clendenning calls Royce, in spite of his commitment to rigorous logic, fundamentally a "philosophical Lohengrin, son of the wandering Parsifal and searcher for the mysterious Grail."

Animals, too, he always loved. He happily ran Judge Head's dogs every morning when he was courting Katharine. In Cambridge he was fond of his cats, memories perhaps of Avon Farm, where a litter of kittens always tumbled about. He called a cat "a fragment of a person," and we should remember that his first childhood venture into fiction personalized a feline, Pussy Blackie. The Royces for a time housed a cageful of Russian rats. Katharine wrote in her diary, "The pets are too sweet. The four baby mice are delightful."Outdoors, the squirrels that darted nervously through the trees of Cambridge always fascinated Josiah. He once created a fictional character suspiciously like himself with blue-gray eyes, who loved chess, smoked all day, was esteemed as a sage, lived "in a mystical chord of contemplation," and, to the point, owned an owl, three parrots, and seven cats.

As for his health, his childhood bout with rheumatic fever may have damaged his heart. But in any case all his life he suffered from asthma, certainly not helped by the animals around the house. It was a family affliction, embracing his mother, his three sisters, and his three sons. He would make light of the attacks, quoting W. S. Gilbert, "Speak *roughly* to your little boy and *beat* him when he wheezes." When sieges were bad, he ignited powdered stramonium leaves and niter on tissue paper and in a dark room above the smoky glow gasped out stories of ghouls and werewolves to the delight of his boys.

In early 1888 Josiah suffered a nervous breakdown. It was six years after his arrival at Harvard, a period in which he struggled against the uncertainties of appointment, wrote three major books and countless lectures, wrestled with a restricted income and a growing family (his second son, Edward, was born in 1886), and learned of the death of two close friends,

George Coale and Edward Rowland Sill. In January he felt depressed, listless, unable to sleep. He called it a "head-weariness" and spoke of a devil in the brain. Like a true Puritan and his mother's child, he experienced a "looking-for of judgment and fiery indignation," but he hoped somehow to find "edifying, instructive" elements in this unusual mental condition. He was Christian again, alone in the Slough of Despond with the burden of the world on his back, desperately seeking the wicket gate of meaning.

The doctor prescribed a long sea voyage, and Josiah arranged a prototype of his mother's 1846 pilgrimage, booking a long passage to primitive, frontier Australia. The choice of destination fulfilled, too, the prophecy of his San Francisco high school story "The Nocturnal Expedition," his moody dream of tragedy on an Australian beach.

Lanman lent him some money, Gilman wrote that he would send the next letter "to a bright Fijian," and in a glowering storm on February 27, 1888, he sailed from Boston on a square-rigged vessel, the *Freeman*. James gave him figs, mineral water, and French novels, all useful for the three months at sea around the Cape of Good Hope to Melbourne. Lanman brought him enough tobacco for the entire voyage, and he smoked it all, "amid the trade-winds, and under the softly flapping canvas," talking astronomy and philosophy with the contemplative Cape Cod captain. One night when the skipper asked him if he thought the stars and the milky way were not in some sense a dream, he answered with a story.

> "There was a countryman," I say, "from Cape Cod, who went to Boston to hear Mark Twain lecture. . . . He was misdirected, so that he heard not Mark Twain, but one of Joseph Cook's Monday Lectures. But he steadfastly believed that he was hearing Mark. So when he went home to Cape Cod, they asked him of Mark Twain's lecture, 'Was it *very* funny?' 'Oh, it was *funny*, yes—it was *funny*,' replies the countryman cautiously, 'but then, you see, it wasn't so damned *funny*.' Even so, Captain," say I, "I teach at Harvard that the world and the heavens, and the stars are all *real*, but not so *damned* real, you see."

He spent seven weeks in Australia, found the climate "very tonic," and felt that he had "recovered my wits pretty completely." "With the winds and the birds of the southern sea came a new life." He took long walks into forests and wild places, such as the Wentworth Valley, with its giant falls. Strangely, in the Blue Mountains he reacted with repulsion, unlike the feelings of joy he remembered in his boyhood California Sierras. But in all instances nature was out there as a force, a healing presence through which his emotions were restored to freshness. Though Oppenheim refers to the growth in him of an "ethics of ecology," he was never an Emersonian mystic seeking immersion and oneness in his surroundings. For him the self and nature stood separate, like the world and the individual or his later worlds of appreciation and description—dependent, interacting, but discrete.

In Australia he puzzled over a frontier society markedly different from what he remembered in California. All cultures, he reasoned, are the products of geography and history. Australia's monotonous and forbidding natural environment shaped not only a self-reliant frontierperson but also a more loyal one. Society down under exhibited a strong sense of community through wide participation in clubs and amateur athletics. Competition was severe, but the relaxed pace of life made it less merciless. Thus unlike Californians' "irresponsibility and rebelliousness," Australians showed "a degree of conservatism, of public spirit, of social discipline, of cheerful conformity to the general will of the community." Australian consciousness, unlike the American suspicion of political authority, expected government to be helpful and involved. Was not this Aussie spirit rather like the happy resignation Royce described in his later psychological biography of John Bunyan? Bunyan, like Royce, had suffered melancholia and despair, recovering only when he learned peace within disruption, a "cheerful conformity to the general will."

He returned on the steamer *Alameda* bound for San Francisco. Aboard was an Australian backwoodsman whom Royce got to know as a man of true self-reliance and at the same time a man of cooperation, dedicated to his neighbors, and so a model of loyalty. It was the kind of frontiersman he craved but seldom observed in America.

So it was California again. He found the family recuperating from his father's recent death in Los Gatos. A wanderer to the end, the elder Josiah had, in spite of declining health, twice left home in his last three years. The son inadvertently epitomized the relationship with his father's wanderlust when in 1884 he wrote his mother a long, six-page letter of news, and then in a cramped afterthought added, "Where is Father?" At the time of the elder Josiah's death, Royce was chiefly sad that he could not be more help to his mother, physically and financially. He took the situation as a lesson that carelessness with health harms more than oneself.

Royce never neglected his family in California. After the death of his father in Los Gatos, his mother moved to San Jose to live with Ruth. She kept in close touch with her son by monthly, sometimes weekly, letters, busy as she was "in the meetings and enterprises of the church, in my Sunday School class of bright and active boys who take care to keep the rust from gathering too thickly up on my head or heart." He addressed her as "Dear little Mother," and she greeted him as "My Precious Josie" or "My ever Precious Son Josie," and once closed with "The Lord's light, and truth, and love be with you, my darling boy." He sent her copies of his professional papers and books, and she responded, "It always seems as if you were talking to me." Once she constructed a small pedestal shrine on which she placed his picture surrounded by leaves and flowers.

In early April 1891 Sarah, seventy-two years old, was in the San Jose post office, perhaps mailing a letter to Josiah, when a heavy man, walking fast, struck her head with his so hard that she reeled to the opposite wall and hit it directly over her eye. Although she suffered a large gash, with bleeding and swelling, she typically made little of the accident, but two days later she became pale and weak, could eat little, and grew increasingly languid. By the end of April she felt shortness of breath,

Sarah Royce. Taken after her husband's death, when she lived in San Jose with or near Ruth. Note the picture of Josiah in the center above her desk. (Courtesy of the Department of Special Collections, University Research Library, UCLA)

cold hands and feet, and a rattling in her throat. A homeo-pathic doctor was called. Brandy and other medications re-vived her, so that in time she even attended church, though with caution. Through the spring and summer she continued to have spells of palpitation, hard breathing, chills, and weak-ness. Once she asked Thomas Barr to come down from Berke-ley, and the old Grass Valley housemate spent the day with her, "so genial and friendly." They must have reminisced, re-calling their church building days together and raising the children in the orchards of Avon Farm.

Her letters to Josiah in those months were reassuring enough that he did not visit her in her illness, though he did send money. In October the doctor wrote that the condition of her heart and spleen made a relapse possible at any time, but the fall term is a particularly hard time to escape a university schedule. With what sadness he must have received the tele-gram from Ruth on November 24, 1891: "Mother died peace-fully at nine-fifteen this evening." Twenty-two years later her daughter Ruth remembered Sarah's "unflinching courage, sturdy faith and self-control, and of their outcome in triumphs for which she sought no occult names and knew no formulas." The triumphs Sarah enjoyed were concentrated in the life of her son.

In spite of illness and tragedy, through most of his thirty-four years at Harvard, Royce's energy often reached remark-able levels. "Painful endeavors" were the price of attainment. "Dissatisfied with what now is, I press on towards what is yet to come." He worked long hours, late into the night, writing lectures for his classes, composing talks for every conceivable public forum, almost always working on some article or book. On top of it all he conducted a prodigious correspondence (six- and seven-page responses were commonplace); one of his recipients, Mark Baldwin, felt his many letters "had a sponta-neity and continued verve which never let up." James was con-stantly impressed with his vigor. "Isn't he a strong man rejoic-ing to run a race?" James wrote; and again, "Royce is working like three men, and thinking like 100."

In addition to all his more serious writing and classwork, in the period before his breakdown he wrote a 130-page piece of fiction called "The Japanese Sword," never published. Against the backdrop of the Civil War, the story expressed his interest in psychic matters, an exploration he shared at the time with William James. The main character, Dr. Caspar, as in the Faust legend, is suspect as a man of science because of his psychic dabblings. But to him a life that is not mysterious "would be like a plain woman without caprices. Unless my mistress baffles me she will not charm me." An acquaintance, Wildham, has been obsessed with a Japanese sword that bears a curse and keeps him from his beloved Beatrice. Caspar, in trying to relieve Wildham of his burden, takes the sword but in the process transfers the curse to himself. Wildham comes to feel that his will has been filched with the weapon, steals it back, and uses it to open an artery and die. In the spirit of his mother, Royce concludes with a biblical reference, Christ casting out devils and speaking of the unclean spirit supplanted by seven that were worse than the first. The story was an echo of his *Berkeleyan* undergraduate essay on Edgar Allen Poe, and it revealed Royce's continuing biblical orientation, his interest in the Civil War and psychic phenomena, his belief in the power of the human will and, by the fact of its writing, in his own enormous energy.

In 1889 Josiah and Katharine moved again. A new residential section was opened near the campus, Norton's Woods, and the Royces, with the help of Katharine's family, bought a lot at 103 Irving Street, where they built a house. It was a lovely, cross-gabled, simple colonial-revival design, with five rooms on the second story, including a nursery and Royce's study, and three more rooms on the third level. From it he could look through the growing trees across Irving Street to the house where young Edward Estlin Cummings, later to be known as e. e. cummings, lived; the boy claimed to have learned about sonnets from his considerate neighbor, Dr. Royce.

In this sheltered tree-shaded spot Josiah and Katharine dwelt for the rest of their lives, raising their children, playing

Royce with William James. At the Jameses' summer place in Chocu-
rua, New Hampshire, in 1903. The friendship between these two
men deeply influenced American thought, and Royce once wrote
James that without him he felt like unbuttered toast. (Courtesy of
the Harvard University Archives)

their music, Katharine writing her stories, Josiah wrestling
with his philosophy. The neighborhood included many friends.
Charles Lanman from around the corner could drop in to
share some passage of the Bhagavad Gita. William James from
two houses away was in and out. Student legends pictured the
two philosophers outside one or the other of their gates freez-
ing their feet in the snow discussing the Absolute. At night if
the rest of the Royce house was dark, James threw stones at
Royce's lighted window to get in. Between their two houses
on Irving Street raged the ageless debate over realism and idealism in its peculiarly American form of pragmatism and absolutism, and when James was away from home, Royce wrote
him, "Cambridge without you is like toast unbuttered."

Santayana once said that, though Royce was born in California, "he had never got used to the sunshine; he had never tasted peace." In this Cambridge land of less sunshine, he flowered, but not because he found peace, for it was not peace but the intellectual fight he sought and cherished. Through the conflict of ideas he found his happiness. In California he had known intellectual stimulation; LeConte and Sill and Moses were hardly nonentities. But he needed more. One of his idols, Immanuel Kant, lived pedantically isolated in a world of books in remote Königsberg. And at a certain level such isolation could have worked for Royce. Instead he was privileged to participate in a golden age of philosophy at Harvard. The question remains, would the result have been substantially different were he not from the American West? Before answering that question, we must assess two events of his early Cambridge years. Early in his career as a philosopher in Harvard's glory days, he wrote a monumental history and a dramatic novel, and through those efforts his ideas about California and the West were to be sharpened and focused.

CHAPTER 9

A History and a Novel

Is it not rather what we expect in men, that they should have numerous strands of experience lying side by side and never compare them with each other?

Eliot, *Middlemarch*

I shall arrive! What time, what circuit first,
I ask not.

Browning, *Paracelsus*

HORACE Elisha Scudder, a small, shy man whose editorial judgments initiated Royce's professional life, played a pivotal role in the Boston publishing firm of Houghton Mifflin. For forty years he significantly influenced the company's choice of authors from William Dean Howells to Woodrow Wilson. By 1883 Scudder probably had heard of Royce, the young Westerner lecturing to wide audiences in Cambridge and stirring up interest by proving God through the existence of error. In any case when Royce sent him the latter lectures under the title *The Religious Aspect of Philosophy*, Scudder accepted them for Houghton Mifflin.

The editor carried an educational arrow in his quiver. Himself writing a history of the United States, he helped his company develop two successful educational series: American Men of Letters, which included James Russell Lowell on Nathaniel Hawthorne; and American Statesmen, which listed Theodore Roosevelt on Gouverneur Morris and Carl Schurz on Henry Clay. Scudder himself edited a third project, individual histories of each state, the American Commonwealth Series. Between 1885 and 1908 he included in his lineup Woodrow Wilson on North Carolina and Brooks Adams on Massachusetts, except that these two projects did not materialize. Rufus

King, however, completed a book on Ohio and Reuben Gold Thwaites wrote on Wisconsin. Otherwise, the twenty authors were primarily local historians, not national names. Similarly, for the California volume Scudder chose William W. Crane, Royce's old friend of the Berkeley Club. Crane, the lawyer and amateur historian, was possibly recommended by Bernard Moses, who also knew Crane well. But not long after Josiah arrived in Cambridge, Crane suddenly died.

Why Scudder did not next ask Moses or Hubert Howe Bancroft or Theodore Hittell, we do not know, except that the series was not intended as professional history. Instead he came to the young man across the Charles, already famed for his western ways, and asked Royce to write the Commonwealth Series volume on the history of California. The offer came to Josiah as a considerable surprise. He had always read history from his school days, reveling in Grote's *History of Greece*, and he certainly nourished personal knowledge of California. He was now committed to philosophy, however, and this book would be a professional detour at best. He wrote Moses for advice, and the response was presumably positive.

As Royce thought about it, the offer began to intrigue him. He openly acknowledged being tempted by the money, and there was some pride involved in writing the first history of California by a native son. What he might say about his state was not inconsiderable. His decision was heavily motivated "by the affection that I should feel for the task" and by the good that might be accomplished in examining "the moral and general significance" of California history. Of course, it would be "a side-work, an amusement of idle hours," but he admitted that such amusements can be "pretty serious things."

In the summer of 1884 the new Harvard instructor threw himself into the job of writing his history of California. He worked in the Harvard Library. Katharine helped take notes on men such as David Broderick and James King (those particular notes were interspersed with children's doodlings). That summer Josiah arranged a research trip back to his home state and went straight to the source, Hubert Howe Bancroft,

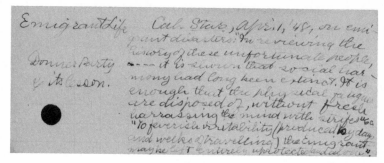

Historical notes. One of the extant note cards (2″ × 5″) taken by Royce while writing his *California*. In this quotation from the California *Star*, what interested him about the Donner Party was the fact that "social harmony had long been extinct." (Courtesy of the Harvard University Archives and Josiah Royce III)

who with his crew of writers was in the midst of his monumental collecting and publishing on the West. Bancroft may have been more chary of his raw material had not Royce's limited agenda seemed no competitive threat to his multivolume work. Royce gained free access to Bancroft's documents packed in a warehouse building on Valencia near Mission Street, south and west of his old route from home to school and not far from the celebrated Woodward's Gardens. Under the guidance of Bancroft's chief researcher and librarian, Henry Lebbeus Oak, he pored through the immense collections of Thomas Oliver Larkin, Mariano Vallejo, and scores of others. "Without Mr. Bancroft's documents," Royce admitted, he would have been "unable to find my way out of the labyrinth." "His [Bancroft's] library is the truly original source here, and my research . . . is at this one most important place but a following of his already beaten trail."

That trail was hardly the idiosyncratic one that Royce would follow, for Bancroft's work was a massive one, the result of mass production appropriate to a nineteenth-century factory. The product should have borne the names of others, especially Henry Oak, who became Royce's good friend and historical confidant. Royce labored more like the lawyer Theodore Hittell, whose history appeared just as Royce was finishing his. Royce referred to Hittell but curiously failed to contact him personally, perhaps the fault of Hittell, a far more private man than Bancroft.

As Royce researched and wrote, his purposes expanded. Before he was through, he saw his history as nothing less than a revelation of the national character. Ultimately it might "serve the true patriot's interest in a clear self-knowledge and in the formation of sensible ideals of national greatness." He understood that there had been wrongdoing in the conquest of California, and his writing might be an atonement for his country's honor. "I have learned, as I have toiled for a while over the sources, to see in these days a process of divinely moral significance."

He restricted his history to ten pivotal years, 1846 to 1856. Extending from the cusp end of this period, his own life and experience lay close. And he took advantage of that fact. When he described California's varied landscape, he included Grass Valley and the Avon Farm views of "frowning higher mountains" and buttes "springing up like young giants." The California climate was healthful, but his own experience exposed a caveat: it prompted "active people to work too steadily, to skip their holidays, and, by reason of their very enjoyment of life, to wear out their constitutions with overwork."

Throughout, his own past echoed. Not too far from where he sat in Bancroft's warehouse, a school lad named Josie once listened to a debate, "Was the Mexican War justified or not?" The same question would now impel his history. From California's standpoint the war and the conquest were indeed unjustified, but beyond that they exposed the American character. The nation had engaged in a morally if not politically indefensible act. When the Bear Flaggers straggled into Sonoma to start a war, their revolt was incited by the false rumors of John Charles Frémont, and thus it was that Frémont became for Royce the butt of the moral problem.

Most historians then and since have allowed that Frémont's call to military action was justifiable, particularly since the fear

of British intervention was rampant. To Royce, however, Frémont's act, predating the arrival of the United States Navy,
could have brought such anarchy to California that England
was more likely than otherwise to have accepted overtures
from the inhabitants for a protectorate. The institution of
guerrilla warfare was not in the best interests of California or
the United States either politically or morally; in it "we can
date the beginning of the degradation, the ruin, and the oppression of the Californian people by our own." And, most
important, the nation lost a striking opportunity to amalgam-
ate a Spanish-speaking province on its own terms without ran-
cor, without bitterness.

Increasingly the documents proved to Royce that the un-
provoked violence, a consequence not of official instructions
but of Thomas Hart Benton's dispatches to Frémont in the
Klamath forests, became "a violation of the laws of nations,
under circumstances of peculiar atrocity." The American consul in Monterey, Thomas O. Larkin, not Frémont, was pursuing the proper national course. Larkin's instructions and actions were geared to the peaceful support of a local movement
for independence from Mexico, which would have led inexo-
rably to annexation by the United States, with far better long-
term consequences. When voluntary conduct is possible, it
must be preferred over coercion. Similarly, in Frémont's acts
and in the official military conquest that followed, Royce saw
the nation typically ambiguous in its desire to conquer but in
its reluctance to assume the role of conqueror. Instead Frémont and the government clothed aggression in the garb of
peaceful intentions and conscientious duty.

How did he reach his conclusion? Initially from the documents. But eventually he was led to the human sources themselves. He decided to take oral histories from John and Jessie
Frémont. William Carey Jones, his Berkeley classmate and colleague, was Frémont's nephew, and through Jones, Royce was
able to set up interviews with the general and his wife, then
living in New York City. In early December 1884 he arrived at
their house on Staten Island and found "a pleasing old gentle-

MS page from interview with the Frémonts, Jessie's comments. For his history of California, Royce interviewed General and Mrs. John Charles Frémont on Staten Island in 1884. He came to distrust the Frémonts' explanation of the conflict, but sought their commentary on the manuscript. Here, to Royce's phrase on Larkin's plan of peaceful acquisition, Jessie lashed out, "Utter nonsense. Fancy England standing by and permitting such slow process—even if the Californians had been willing—which they were not." (Courtesy of the Bancroft Library, University of California, Berkeley.)

man, quiet, cool, self-possessed." Jessie, he wrote his mother, "is not so well preserved in her old age as is the General. She is extremely vain now and garrulous. She could talk of nothing but her own family, and the 'glorious policy of my father.'" The young interviewer's questions were to the point: instead of starting a war, was not Frémont bound by the government's instructions to Consul Larkin, which had been shown to Frémont and which called for a more peaceable course? The Frémonts denied the existence of any such directive. For Royce the moment was a keen delight, for with Oak's permission, he was carrying the document itself in his pocket. This disingenuous act, in which Royce seemed to relish catching Frémont in a lie, was instrumental in his disenchantment with the general and his wife. That disillusion was not unique, for as Royce was well aware, California's electorate, those who had been "liberated," disavowed their own "liberator" in the election of 1856, giving Frémont only some 20,000 votes of nearly 110,000 cast. But whatever his internal relish, Royce conducted the interviews in a highly professional manner, allowing the Frémonts a chance to amend, read proofs, and offer rebuttals.

Royce's ruminations on the conquest went beyond the drunkenly tragic Bear Flaggers, the Gallant Captain, and the Mexican War. They indicted a nation and a generation. In an oft-quoted passage the historian addressed his fellow citizens of the 1880s, a people beginning to tangle with overseas markets, acquisitions such as Alaska, and Chinese exclusion.

> It is to be hoped that this lesson [the conquest of California], showing us as it does how much of conscience and even of personal sincerity can coexist with a minimum of effective morality in international undertakings, will some day be once more remembered; so that when our nation is another time about to serve the devil, it will do so with more frankness and will deceive itself less by half-unconscious cant. For the rest, our mission in the cause of liberty is to be accomplished through a steadfast devotion to the cultivation of our own inner life, and not by going abroad as missionaries, as conquerors, or as marauders, among weaker peoples.

As the manuscript progressed to the period of military rule between the conquest and admission, Royce asked similarly broad questions. He called it "a time of doubts, of problems, of complaints, and of weariness." In such moments the American nature could be at its best—moderate, self-controlled, and astute in the design of new communities. Unfortunately, however, this period was dominated by the discovery of gold, a phenomenon that naturally fascinated the boy from Grass Valley.

Royce treated the gold rush in broad sociological fashion. Along with the technology of mining, the establishment of justice and order, and the treatment of foreigners, he examined domestic life, marital relations, and the behavior of women in the emerging mining society. It is perhaps natural that he thought to ask his own mother, Sarah, to write her memoirs, to put in writing all those tales he had heard as a boy from that strong woman who had made him what he was. She responded with a book-length detailed account of her months on the trail in 1849 and her years in Weaverville, Sacramento, and San Francisco, regrettably stopping just as the family arrived in Grass Valley.

He received the manuscript in December of 1884 and was gratefully impressed. "It is so straightforwardly and sensibly, and withal so earnestly written, that it is in itself a very valuable and readable document, apart from its use to me. I shall make it a point to get it printed sometime. . . . It will help me meanwhile much." Royce used the material extensively and openly in his history, proving as it did the intensification of religious steadfastness on the plains journey, the forging of community through a few lonesome families, and the vital role religion played by asserting public duty in early San Francisco. He understandably dedicated the entire work "To my mother, a California pioneer of 1849."

In the gold rush Royce found California "to be morally and socially tried as no other American community ever has been tried." Out of that explosion, the state and its restless population exhibited "both the true nobility and the true weakness of our national character." The nobility was seen in a divided population that successfully dealt with the hatreds between the North and the South through the kind of debates he had heard on the streets of Grass Valley; in the activities of women who injected family and religious values into a raw society, as with his own mother and her Christian Church circles; and especially in the average American's "instinctive cleverness" at self-government.

Royce warned, however, that Californians' "marvelous political talent" must be seen against two evidences of weakness: civic irresponsibility and a local manifestation of the diseased national feeling toward foreigners. Both of these tendencies allowed orderly, friendly life to degenerate into violence. Although miners in a spirit of compromise and good humor bound themselves into "little republics," their camps were devoid of broader civic responsibility, and they consequently endured years of disorder.

The social fabric needed mending. With bitterness Royce described the cruelty and ineffectiveness of lynch law in the mines and pointed out the hypocrisy of those who whined about law and order but refused to be taxed for jails. As for foreigners, Royce wrote, "You cannot build up a prosperous and peaceful community so long as you pass laws to oppress and torment a large resident class of the community." Foreigners were kept by law and vigilantism in fear and misery, a condition he had seen close at hand on Main Street in Grass Valley and Powell Street in San Francisco.

Disorder served in the end to teach social responsibility. Those fearful fires that his family witnessed in San Francisco in the early 1850s plus his own memories of the bright new fire engines in Grass Valley preceded sounder buildings, safer docks, more organized fire departments. In the same way a society typified by overexcitement, self-absorption, extravagance, and nervous strain was in time balanced by family life and church-oriented circles. The vigilance committees of 1851 and particularly 1856 eventually rooted out the social apathy and public carelessness that surrounded them.

In short, the state took a trip through the slough of despond. Those difficult years included the Land Act of 1851 (requiring all existing titles to be confirmed by a commission). Royce felt the act ("lamentably legalized anarchy") expressed "our natural meanness and love of good order in one." It was mean because it singled out the Mexicans to justify the land titles which they had been promised in the Treaty of Guadalupe Hidalgo. Good order was the American propensity for legal clarity.

In this period of despond the new state politicians such as John Bigler, David Broderick, and William Gwin helped little; they were "too selfish to be wise." In the end, however, there was enough feeling for the whole, enough of that binding element that changed the selfish into the communal, to produce a living, dynamic community.

> It is the State, the Social Order, that is divine. We are all but dust save as this social order gives us life. When we think it our instrument, . . . we call it sordid, degraded, corrupt, unspiritual, and ask how we may escape from it forever. But if we turn again and serve the social order, and not merely ourselves, we soon find that what we are serving is simply our own highest spiritual destiny in bodily form. It is never truly sordid or corrupt or unspiritual; it is only we that are so when we neglect our duty.

Seldom has a history led to such lofty conclusions. California's ten formative years were not just the germ of a future, not just a parable for the American character; they were lessons in the proper ordering of human society.

The critical response to *California* was not that glowing. An unsigned review in the *Overland Monthly* was vicious (some have thought it was Bernard Moses, but his friendship with Royce would seem to belie it). The book was here described as "contract work, done under pressure," without unity "except in its uniformity of sermonizing reproof of Americans." The anonymous reviewer found the censure of Frémont and California frontiersmen excessive and unproved. And in the end, "both as literature and as history, it is, on the whole, a failure." Sprinkled through the review were words like "immaturity," "flippancy," "diffuseness," and "unidiomatic English," and it concluded with a patronizing nod: "Defects like this . . . will naturally disappear with longer experience in writing history; and we advert to them for Professor Royce's good."

Shortly before in the *Nation* Royce unfavorably compared Theodore Hittell's new history with Bancroft's emerging work, and now Royce assumed that the *Overland* reviewer was the incensed Hittell. In a letter to his friend and the journal's editor, Milicent Shinn, Royce revealed little resentment. Henry Oak in the next month's issue of the *Overland* firmly supported Royce's position on Frémont and affirmed the book "both as literature and as history" to be "a very perfect piece of work," superior to anything yet done. William A. Dunning in the *Political Science Quarterly* was more guarded. "If only the excellence of the author's literary style were at all proportionate to the captiousness of his criticism, his book would easily take rank as a classic."

Royce's interest in history was now too deep to be easily deflected. The rebukes he suffered from reviewers led to more activity, not less. He corrected a minor detail in the *California* by a letter to the editor of the *Overland*. He contributed a series of biographies on figures in California history to *Appleton's Cyclopaedia*. He edited lengthy documents and letters by George H. Fitch, William Coleman, William Tecumseh Sherman, John B. Montgomery, George Bancroft, and James Buchanan in a series of contributions to *Century*. At the same time he wrote five lengthy reviews of the emerging Bancroft and Hittell volumes. In these he championed Bancroft's sound documentary evidence and Hittell's readability while castigating Bancroft's failure to credit his coauthors and Hittell's failure to profit from Bancroft's collection of sources.

In this matter, as so often, Royce revealed himself as a fighter. He poured out articles and letters that became an extended rebuttal to his critics, clarifying questions and adding proofs. Most of the debate revolved around his interpretation of the conquest. Frémont died in July 1890, and in an *Atlantic* article Royce was quick to assess the general's life and work. Royce pronounced Frémont a "faithful knight and hero" with "winning eyes and gentle voice," one who "possessed all the qualities of genius except ability." He was "a creature escaped from a book, wandering about in a real world when he was made for dreamland." Royce again charged Frémont with refusal to take the ordered and more desirable course of neutrality, conciliation, and ultimate annexation with less fighting and with fewer resentments. "General Frémont was simply *not* the conqueror of California. All that he did . . . was of no effect except to alienate its people."

Although Frémont's death might have dashed the hope that the general would disclose anything more on the California conquest, a twelve-page double-columned article appeared in the April 1891 *Century*, "edited" by Jessie from the notes of her deceased husband. In it Frémont's military actions were justified by the threat of British occupation of California. Furthermore, the article contended that Frémont was given the power to act in his secret instructions for the 1845 scientific expedition. When Lieutenant Archibald Gillespie found him on the Oregon border, the unofficial message from his father-in-law Benton showed that conciliation was "no longer practicable" and in any case would have been "in conflict with our own instructions." Frémont dismissed one part of Gillespie's dispatches (the official orders to Larkin) and concentrated on the other (the letter from Benton), "a trumpet," which "made me know distinctly that at last the time had come when England must not get a foothold; that we *must be first*. I was to *act*, discreetly but positively."To support his position, Frémont submitted an 1886 memorandum from George Bancroft, the former secretary of the navy, then retired in Rhode Island. In it Bancroft denied much contemporary fear of England, but he admitted that, if he had been in Frémont's place, he would have felt bound to do what he could to promote the purpose of the president, the possession of California.

In the same issue, Royce printed Secretary of State Buchanan's letter to Larkin (the Gillespie dispatch). Royce added an editorial note in which he pointed to this document as the *only* official dispatch received by Frémont, the one Josiah as interviewer had held in his pocket. Buchanan indicated that, though the government wished no foreign control over California, still "this government has no ambitious aspirations to gratify and no desire to extend our Federal system over more territory than we already possess, unless by the free and spontaneous wish of the independent people of adjoining territories."

The *Century* readers were wearying of the California controversy, so Royce was forced to turn to the *Nation*, where in May 1891 (while completing his *Spirit of Modern Philosophy*, contemplating six articles on Goethe, and considering an offer to move from Harvard to Stanford) he offered his final words on the subject. He protested that George Bancroft's comments did not change the picture, that every agent of the United States had orders to conciliate the Mexicans, that cooperation was thwarted by Frémont's false reports and irregular warfare, and that the letter of the retired George Bancroft was sprinkled with errors in memory. For further evidence Royce quoted verbatim the dispatch of Bancroft to Commodore Sloat, once more ordering conciliation. The truth was that Frémont "lawlessly thwarted [orders] for his own glory. . . . I should myself never think of attacking the Frémont legend so often, were it not so unsubstantially immortal. I shall rejoice, indeed, if ever the pale ghost ceases to walk in broad daylight. The twilight regions of our historical consciousness in this country will probably never be rid of it." And with these words he closed his public comment on John Charles Frémont and the conquest of California.

Royce's preoccupation with the role of Frémont lasted for six years. Throughout he admitted Frémont's value as a scientist and explorer. Robert Underwood Johnson, editor of the *Century*, remembered Royce's "genuine admiration for the character of Frémont's work and reports" and urged Royce to write an article on Frémont as an explorer. But on Frémont as the soldier and diplomat, Josiah vacillated between giving the "conqueror" the benefit of the doubt and, at the other extreme, applying the "thumb-screw" to "the deceiver." Something inexplicable motivated Royce in his unwillingness at least to assume Frémont's good intentions, even if thoroughly mistaken. Why did he not understand, to use his own later words, "the art of honoring your opponent's loyalty?" Andrew Rolle, the western psychohistorian, has suggested that we may be observing the psychological overreaction of one strong will (Frémont) to the authoritarianism of an equally strong will (Royce). If so, it must be added that Royce throughout his life loved to explore differences and heartily championed the clash of minds. He taught that way and he lived that way, particularly in gargantuan debates with Francis Abbot and William James, his colleagues at Harvard.

Nor was Royce's tirade stirred up in a mental vacuum. Henry Oak by correspondence was agreeing with Royce. Edward Sill wondered what General Sherman after reading *California* would do to Royce on the field of battle. Milicent Shinn, his friend and *Overland* editor, almost dared him: "Sometimes you simply *can't* unseat a legend, no matter how much you show it up." His editor, Robert Johnson, was encouraging him with his own judgments on Frémont's position as "exasperatingly Jesuitical" and "as an endeavor to carry water on both shoulders and on the head as well."

Frémont touched the deepest chords of Royce's ethical concerns. The "gallant captain" was admirable enough in his practicality and his strong will and in a professed loyalty to his nation, but like many self-proclaimed patriots, his loyalty lacked moral dimension, was weak in loyalty to loyalty. He disobeyed his government's orders, conspired with Senator Benton in a family plot, and acted above all for his own personal glory. Frémont thought that a new community could be built on conquest, and Royce's whole life was constructed on a radically different assumption.

Judged by the standards of his day or by the basic canons of scholarship, Royce as a historian of California comes off rather well. For errors of detail his *California* is occasionally vulnerable, especially in the introduction on pre-American California, the section in which he was little concerned and for which he claimed no scholarship. In it he underestimated Indian uprisings against the missions, underplayed the Monterey stay of Commodore Thomas ap Catesby Jones in 1846, and had the

Donner party's Reed banished on foot rather than horseback. He also confused the number and nature of the prisoners taken by the Bear Flaggers. And he wholeheartedly accepted J. Tyrwhitt Brooks ("a perfectly trustworthy observer") as a prime source for life in the mines, even fascinated enough with the name Tyrwhitt to use it in his story "The Japanese Sword." We now know that Brooks's journal was a hoax, revealed fifty years afterward by its author (Henry Vizetelly), but the entire historical profession at the time believed in Brooks.

Against these details must be placed the body of the work. Over and over Royce's reverence for documentation shone clearly. "The purpose has been throughout to write from the sources," and by sources he meant a range of newspapers, letters, and diaries. He called his historical bent "my respect for thoroughness," and it lay behind his enthusiasm for Bancroft's work. As he was writing his *California*, he expressed to Henry Oak the anguish of the careful documentary historian. "It is fearfully hard to tell the truth in these things. Again and again I write what I think I have just learned from a document or book, and, looking again at my source, have to tear up my MS. in disgust."

In style, his work is not professional history. He often descended to sarcasm: "Providence, again, is known to be opposed to every form of oppression; and grabbing eleven leagues of land is a great oppression. And so the worthlessness of Mexican land-titles is evident." He argued from analogy: "If we desired to steal our neighbor's fine horse, why should we first coax him into confinement and then scourge him with whips in his stall, to make him break his bones?" His metaphors were occasionally overdrawn: "The devil's instrument it actually proved to be, . . . and we have got our full share of the devil's wages for our use of it [Land Act of 1851]." He editorialized and personalized his arguments in ways the modern historian might envy but never dream of doing.

Yet the final stylistic impact was one of grandness, of an exciting mind caught up in the joy of intellectual pursuit. His phrasing betrayed that exhilaration: "April and May are the spendthrift months of wealthy nature." The year 1849 was "the boyish year of California." Speculative investors "will be destroyed like flies in the autumn." Sometimes overdrawn, his similes were more often apt: "California would have been ready to drop into our basket like a mellow apple." He was never bashful in drawing upon his wealth of reading. His mother and father would have been proud to find how ready the Bible was for him. From it he viewed the Mexican War through the Old Testament story of Ahab coveting Naboth's vineyard. Again, the population "was full of Jonahs, . . . fleeing over seas and deserts." Elsewhere wild grapes and manna and ravens were scattered in the wilderness. Thucydides and Aristotle were also there. And so were Jonathan Swift and Lewis Carroll (no less than the Boojum from *The Hunting of the Snark*). The result was a work of undoubted literary merit.

Royce's venture in history was truly remarkable. He presaged a great deal of later historiography, a tribute to the breadth of his mind. His book could easily be described as new social history. "The social condition has been throughout of more interest to me than the individual men, and the men themselves of more interest than their fortunes." Thus in the work there is no biography of Frémont but rather a critique of Frémont's actions and how they muddied future racial relations; there is no life of James King, the martyred editor, but an exploration of how King's death changed the reform consciousness of San Francisco.

Furthermore, Royce was an ecologist in that he conceived of life as interacting with an environment. It was the land and its resources, not simply political decisions, that determined patterns of legal title and settlement. In an address to the National Geographic Society in 1898, "A Psychological Study of the Relations of Climate and Civilization," he continued an interest, first explored in his *California*, in "how the physical features of the Pacific Coast may be expected to mould our national type." In part, he said, the mild climate led to an intimacy with nature and ultimately to a habit of personal independence. Physical features encouraged a developed sense of

place. Thus geography fed psychology. True, in his own life
he abandoned his place, his West, for the East, as Bernard
DeVoto would do later, rather than addressing the East from
a base in the West, as did Charles Shinn or Vernon Louis Parrington. But this was part of his ambiguity about California
and his love-hate relation with it. Whatever his personal hegira, he always understood the fundamental importance of
place and rootedness in a well-ordered community.

Seen as a sociologist, Royce recognized racial issues. His
sympathetic treatment of Mexican society (perhaps carried to
an extreme as free, careless, and charming) was at least an en-
lightened attitude on race. Not that Royce did not share his
generations' elitism in racial matters. In California "the better
families of the community were superior to the average Mexicans." Elsewhere he used the term "nigger." Still, his more
broad-minded feelings were reflected later in his life when,
against a tide of national nativism, he publically supported free
immigration.

More broadly, Royce's work may be compared to a major
strain of modern sociological history that is built on Max Weber's writings on collective consciousness (the collective mores
of Protestantism, for example, support the presuppositions of
capitalism)—what the more recent historian calls mentalities.
In such thinking biography is eschewed in favor of a more
embracing social entity, and Royce was on an early version of
that track. He saw the struggle for order transcending the conflicting and confused voices of individuals. Vigilante justice
was more than meetings and hangings; it was no less than "the
confession of the past sin of the whole community" and as
such held communal meaning.

Like the modern cultural anthropologist, Royce was concerned with the sources of law and disorder. His emphasis on
social order is not surprising, since he came to maturity in the
1880s, the period in which the modern historian Robert Wiebe
found America's self-directed communities faltering before
centralized government while personal identification by occupation replaced identification through community. In Royce's

mind early Californians created the very forms that Royce's own society was losing, and he might in consequence have championed the founders of community in California more than he did the perpetuators of self-reliance. The builders of the commonwealth for Royce were not the entrepreneurs and businessmen, as important as they were to him, but the men and women who were bringing traditional forms to a raw, unkempt life. The new society Royce championed was a renewal not a denial of the old; ontogeny recapitulated phylogeny. And that society of close-knit community had been undermined by the frontier and was now under attack again by the modern marketplace, factory, and city.

Royce knew that any form of community may act immorally. The vigilance committee of 1856, for example, for all of its beneficial social effects, was itself no more than a "Business Man's Revolution," a group of entrepreneurs furthering its own economic interests. This hard-headed concept of the vigilance committee has taken a firm hold on subsequent historical interpretation.

Worthy of the modern French *Annales* school of historians, Royce foresaw the modern carryover from technology to culture, notably in underlining the social effects of mining techniques. The shovel and the pan allowed pure individualism; they precluded "secure progress in the organized life of the camps." The miner's cradle was an agent of social change, creating "a collection of mutually more or less independent, but inwardly united bands." Later mining techniques "acted indirectly on society, as a check to the confusion and disorder," finally bringing men together in companies and more complex social relations. The sluice thus became the "basis for the social life of a civilized community."

As a budding philosopher, Royce saw history on a grand scale. Beyond his facts lay an overarching world of meaning. Even his obsession with Frémont's role in the conquest was in the end a matter of authority and damaged race relations; the gold-rush society was an early study in the search for what he would later call the beloved community. Still, through his philosophy emerged remarkable premonitions of a social science history whose canons would not capture most historians for generations. He saw mining camps as societies contending with technological change. He realized the importance of a sense of place, of technology as a factor in social flux, of collective consciousness, of the limitations on individualism. The writing of his *California*, which philosophers see as a digression, earned Royce a significant place in western historiography.

The summer after the publication of *California*, the young assistant professor unobtrusively began to write a novel. Katharine apparently helped him, but she was pregnant with their second son, Edward, and thus Royce's explanation for digressing, "I think it has something to do with earning my living," takes on added meaning. That year he wrote a friend in California, "I am struggling very hard nowadays to earn a decent living in an expensive town, on a very insufficient salary." Of course, there is a tendency for academics to try their hands at fiction. Even that same summer Henry Adams and Adolph Bandelier were so engaged. Intellectuals such as Helen Hunt Jackson and Ignatius Donnelly also come to mind, but these latter had social purposes, not very obvious with Royce.

For Josiah literature was hardly a stranger. He dabbled in short stories from the time he was eight years old. His undergraduate Charter Day oration extolled the modern novel. George Eliot never ceased to attract him. Why not apply his newly acquired insights into California history to a fictional mode? It might deepen a reader's thinking about his own society, just as George Eliot's work helped understand English nineteenth-century life. It was, he said, "a spider-web of a job."

The historical question of Royce's novel was already embodied in his *California*—whether land holdings should be large, as in the traditional rancho, or be broken into smaller parcels. He considered the issue fundamental to California's development. The section in his history dealing with the Sacramento squatter riots of 1850 was the only portion of his book that he extracted and expanded for a separate article in the *Overland*, and he would eventually use that essay for one of his *Studies of Good and Evil* (1898). Now it would be the centerpiece of his story. He planned a more literary title but eventually chose one closer to the geography and the history: *The Feud of Oakfield Creek: A Novel of California Life.*

The story begins in the autumn of 1882 with the troubled marriage of Tom and Margaret Eldon. "Pale, graceful, and dark-eyed," Tom was the weak son of Alonzo Eldon, a robust magnate who lived in a Nob Hill mansion. Margaret, the strongest character of the book, an intelligent rich widow, "thoughtful, soft-voiced, self-contained, and a perfect manager of other people," married Tom without realizing that he was still courting Ellen Escott. Ellen killed herself over the affair, and when Tom's duplicity was exposed, the tragedy soured the new marriage.

Ellen's father, Alf Escott, was a Bohemian college professor who criticized his students unsparingly but "was so simple and sincere about it that the best ones seldom took offense." He and Tom's father, Alonzo, were once bosom friends. As old Californians they fought the Paiutes together, epitomes of loyalty to one another and to their cause. Now their children's conflict further sharpened a clash that began over Eldon's desire to build a Medici fortune rather than be concerned, like Escott, with the common people who made such affluence possible. Ironically, the robber-baron Eldon assuaged his conscience with a closet attachment to the teachings of Henry George, yearning for a society in which opulence like his own would be impossible. He was a torn man—an industrialist courting socialism, a committer of mean acts wanting to be remembered for kindly ones, a pioneer in the process of losing one society and finding another. He lived alone, using only a corner of his big house and dreaming that Margaret, his daughter-in-law, would someday give it life. Like California, he had abandoned community and now searched for atonement.

The estranged Eldon and Escott each owned land between

Mount Diablo and the Contra Costa hills, and here is where the feud of Oakfield Creek developed. The area was claimed by small squatters, including Alf Escott (patterned in his idealism after the leader of the Sacramento squatters). Alonzo Eldon bought title to the land through a *sobrante*, an ill-defined Spanish grant, and now threatened to develop the area, charge the squatters correspondingly exorbitant prices to buy, or evict them.

Through complicated subplots—including a wandering widower, William Harold, who in the end wins Margaret's affections, and a flamboyant, corrupt newspaper editor, Louis Boscowitz, who fronts for Eldon—the story winds to its tragic denouement. That action includes the Brotherhood of the Noble Rangers, squatters defending their rights under a higher law in the pattern of the Sacramento Settlers' Association or the San Francisco vigilance committees. In the end forty settlers resist the approach of Eldon and his men, and in the consequent shooting, old Escott, Eldon's son, and four others die.

This final scene is a virtual replay of the events in Sacramento in 1850, and they are reminiscent, too, of the Mussell Slough incident (May 11, 1880), which Frank Norris recreated in *The Octopus* (1901). Norris followed Royce's path through the University of California, where he was also influenced by the Darwinian philosophy of Joseph LeConte. His characters were victims in naturalistic, evolutionary traps, while Royce's principals stood in moral dilemmas, facing conflicting loyalties between higher law or immediate needs, between family or communal attachments; the ultimate values were unshakable, and they had to include loyalty to a cause beyond the self.

Among other things, the novel points up Royce's feelings about women. He harbored some sentiments that would delight Owen Wister or any cowboy novelist. "You don't know," said Ellen to Margaret, "you women, how such things come to pass among men." Yet, knowing both a dominant mother and a talented wife, Josiah was never ambiguous about the importance of women. In the history, women—the catalysts of family, church, school, and local attachments—stand as strong counterweights to social disruption and mob disorder. *The Feud* explored Margaret's complexity far beyond any narrowly Victorian concept of womankind. She was fallible, struggling with moral problems such as love outside of marriage, and she earned her goodness, unlike the men of the story, for whom moral dilemmas were given and clear cut. It is Margaret who questioned the stereotype of women as creatures governed chiefly by feeling, and she concluded, "Men are the least rational beings on earth."

Reviews were mixed. The *Holborn Review* was vicious. In a two-sentence notice, it snorted, "This is an unwholesome story, and it is unformed and sometimes stilted in style. Californian life should yield some literature of a higher quality than such a book." The *Nation* went to the reverse extreme: "The scenes and the mechanism of the story are so perfectly flavored with the soil. . . . The quiet strength and delicacy, . . . the plain, straightforward, vigorous style that counts for so much in the admirableness of the whole work; . . . the novel is sterling throughout." The *Dial* called it "unbearably prolix" but also "gracefully written," with local color "effectively applied." When Gilman received his copy of *The Feud*, he wrote Royce, "Among the innumerable publications which our former Fellows have given to the world, this is, I believe, the first Romance."

Whatever the reviews, Royce found that a California novel, like California history, was an effective tool for a moral purpose. He learned that history "talks back," offers documents that must be coped with, and never "stands still to be counted." He might have said that literature, as he said of philosophy, is "submissive and plastic." The story of an unhappy marriage and the background of California squatters was molded into a morality of duty and desire, what one commentator has called "a perspective on identity and morality." It was the collective cause, the fight of Escott's neighbors in the land dispute, that finally brought changes in individual consciousness. In some

respects the history and the novel may be seen as curious de-
tours in the life of a young Harvard philosopher. The two
books, however, grew straight out of his California back-
grounds and merely explored in other forms his life's deepest
preoccupations.

CHAPTER 10

The West as Metaphysics

> A light
> Will struggle through these thronging words at last,
> As in the angry and tumultuous West
> A soft star trembles through the drifting clouds.
> These are the strivings of a spirit which hates
> So sad a vault should coop it, and calls up
> The past to stand between it and its fate.
>
> Browning, *Paracelsus*

WHILE Royce was writing his history and his novel, he lectured about his native state to all manner of Cambridge audiences, including the Daughters of the American Revolution—reiterating the mistakes in the California conquest, painting the disorders of gold-rush society. Townspeople and students packed Harvard's Sanders Theater to hear him. He relished his role as an unpolished Westerner in the effete East. It was as if he could not let go. The West was his amulet, whose inscription exorcised the ghost of his desertion, or his albatross, whose dangling weight both hindered and released him. He was bound to his past but was now justified in publicly damning it. As he later wrote of Spinoza's excommunication, the break left him "free to criticise the life that no longer enchains him."

In one such lecture he berated the wild "mischievous tendency" of the fur trade, especially in Canada. "Civilized" settlement, however, was not that much better. Which of them "pleased God best, I know not; and it seems to me that of such things history cannot well treat until after the judgment day." But Royce always knew, if not what pleased God, at least what side he himself was on. California may have been won "by the

sword or by deceit," but in the end it was families, represent-
ing "the presence and the power of spiritual things," that
righted the situation. He could assign merit to Frémont only
because his report of 1843–44 successfully guided emigrant
groups.

Coterminously, as we have seen, he was building the structure of his philosophy. In 1885, for example, he corrected the
final proofs of *The Religious Aspect of Philosophy* while he was
still working on the history of California and publishing the
article on the squatter riots of 1850 in Sacramento. In the philosophy there were metaphors of foxes, wildcat mines and
journeys beyond the deserts. "A child born in one of our far
western settlements," he wrote, can still sense the community
and "reverence the oldest deserted, weather-beaten, rotting
log-cabin of the place, with its mud chimney crumbling to
dust, quite as much as a modern Athenian child may reverence
the ruins of the Parthenon." Religion was defined in frontier
terms as practical and emotional as well as theoretical: "It
teaches us to do, to feel, and to believe." He demanded the
right to criticize "as fearlessly, as thoroughly, and as skeptically
as may be." William James called this book "redolent of the
smell of the earth."

At the same time, philosophy was crossing over into his
purposes for writing about the Sacramento squatters: "to feel
the difference between the healthy and diseased states of social
activity." He deduced a practical moral from those riots: we
"cannot hope to reach the divine by sulking in the bush. . . .
[P]atient loyalty to the actual social order is the great reformer's first duty." His conversation with the past was informing
his conversation with eternity. The process was analogous to
what he would later call the doctrine of Signs and Interpretation. "The present interprets the past to the future. At each
moment of time the results of the whole world's history up to
that moment are, so to speak, summed up and passed over to
the future for its new deeds of creation and of interpretation."

As his philosophy continued to develop in later years, his
interest in California, though no longer expressed directly in

publications, remained strong. There were few gaps in his involvement in the intellectual life of his home state. In 1891 he reluctantly turned down the offer of a chair in philosophy at Stanford University. By then it was a sense of duty to Harvard that was the chief reason, not a lack of desire to return to California. His interest in Palo Alto again surfaced in his support for E. A. Ross when Stanford fired the sociologist in 1900. Berkeley called Royce back on many occasions, notably in 1895, when the university welcomed their most distinguished graduate to a glittering discussion on the existence of God; in the summer of 1902, when he taught a course on metaphysics and reveled "in youthful memories"; and again in 1914, when he was entertained by the Riebers and lectured the summer school and the Philosophical Union. He spent much of his sabbatical leave of 1903 in California, and on two occasions (1911 and 1916) declined his alma mater's efforts to bring him home again. Though he did not himself permanently return, he injected into California's educational life one after another of his students—A. O. Lovejoy, Charles Rieber, John Boodin, Jacob Loewenberg—as well as participating in presentations there with former students such as Sidney Mezes and James Mark Baldwin. For a time he was a corresponding member of the California Historical Society. His 1902 lectures on provincialism, still drawing heavily on his boyhood, were reprinted in *Race Questions, Provincialism, and Other American Problems* (1908), along with his 1898 talk to the National Geographic Society entitled "The Pacific Coast: A Psychological Study of Influence."

When his student Jacob Loewenberg was hired for the new philosophy department at Berkeley, Royce took him along on a Caribbean voyage and, at sea day after day, conducted with the young philosopher a miniseminar on California and his own history of it. Then "out would pour a profusion of items which for lack of space were not included in the text." This was more than twenty years after he had written his *California*. He wrote his wife of Loewenberg's plan to offer in Berkeley a course on Royce, "the philosophy of a native son." It would be "given officially upon the very spot where once my feet were deeply impressed in the mud of each successive rainy season." During his California visit of 1914 he talked to his old Berkeley Club not on his philosophy but on Edward McGowan, the "jolly villain" victim of the great San Francisco Vigilance Committee. Again, as we will see, at the very end of his life, receiving the warm plaudits of the philosophy profession, Royce devoted most of his acknowledgment to his childhood and youth in California. His western experience composed a readily accessible part of his life, like an aquifer, a submerged but enduring sustenance.

Yet in his purely philosophical work, there was a notable absence of direct allusion to the American West. Royce went out of his way to use other illustrations when personal western ones would have worked. He wrote of isolated individuals who might still learn self-possession through self-surrender and used as his example lighthouse keepers instead of those isolated prospectors he had known in Grass Valley. Frémont himself or western communities like San Francisco resorting to mob violence would have answered just as well as Cromwell and Caesar when he described human wills meeting opposing wills and thereby reviving "primal solipsism." "It is the fate of life to be restless," he wrote, and he could have added scores of examples from his western memories, certainly the experience of his own parents on the plains. The vigilance committee of 1856 could have been the "right wing of any elaborate social order" or "the metaphysic of the party of good order." His mother would have exemplified devotion to an ideal as effectively as his choice of a little girl waiting for a king outside a palace wall. Though there are exceptions, he passed over opportunities on all sides.

The customs of philosophical writing might explain the Western lapse. A better justification, however, lies in Royce's challenge to himself as an intellectual, and especially an emerging eastern intellectual. During the early 1890s he eschewed his role as a scholar-historian, and in the period in which he sought a regular rather than an interim position at Harvard, he assumed the full-time role of intellectual. If there is a distinction between the scholar, who collects and documents, and the intellectual, who judges and interprets, Royce was moving between these worlds, something like the reverse transition David Hume made a century earlier from philosophy to history. But Royce, unlike Hume, established his name in philosophy during the period in which American philosophy was being professionalized. He wrote philosophical history, but he could not sail a strictly philosophical course by tacking into the waters of personal history. Utilizing his own story was not appropriate for a neoprofesssional philosopher in Harvard's golden age.

Then too Royce, Europeanized and Easternized, revered philosophers like Lotze and Wundt, ivy-enveloped professors, immersed in their texts, removed from their societies, presumably transcending their own transient times and places. Royce saw these men as scientists, and science functioned in a world beyond conflicting cultures.

At the same time Royce engaged in a discourse with his adopted eastern audience. Though he was perfectly willing to take advantage of a popular interest in the West and play that role for campus gatherings, philosophy was something else. The West was, after all, barren for him as a budding philosopher. That "blind and stupid and homeless generation of selfish wanderers" that he knew in the West, with a very few exceptions such as LeConte and Sill, did not stand high in his ratings; he would hardly have expected a western constituency for his philosophy.

He made his stand at Harvard. It was his institutional platform, surrounded by an elitist society to which he was not born. He was the social ugly duckling, and his background was only minimally acceptable. As an academic subdiscipline in Cambridge, the West remained unrecognized. Frederick Jackson Turner was not called to Harvard till 1910, well after Royce established himself as a philosopher. By then the West became nostalgia for Royce, and the opportunity to use its images freshly and directly in his writings had passed.

Nevertheless, throughout his philosophy the dialogue with his own past became internalized. On some such threshold of awareness the West worked in Royce. George Santayana once said of his teacher and colleague, "He seemed to view everything in relation to something else that remained untold." "Every philosophy," wrote Alfred North Whitehead, "is tinged with the coloring of some secret, imaginative background, which never emerges explicitly in its train of reasoning." The West for Royce was one of those inner voices that he was not recovering or reconstructing but rather transfiguring into its philosophical forms. These remnants were exposed in his rhetoric and style, in his arguments and ideas, in implicit assumptions, and in reactions to his cultural context. "The work of memory," said Susan Sontag, "collapses time." The work of Royce collapsed his West into a subconscious metaphor.

Royce's style was highly personalized and usually in the form of the original lecture. In *The Spirit of Modern Philosophy*, unlike his books that preceded and followed, he even employed frequent contractions—it's, that's, isn't, shouldn't, I'm, can't—a practice generally frowned on in formal writing of the day. Like Ezra Pound and other stylistic rebels, he reached for a freer, more personal, more honest, more colloquial stance. Though he abandoned this particular technique, he never ceased to use informal interjections—well, now, yes, I know.

He wrote as if he were speaking, and he loved to talk, even sermonize. In childhood he argued interminably with his sisters. As an established philosopher, words poured out of him tirelessly. "The tap once turned on, out flowed the stream of systematic disquisition, one hour, two hours, three hours of it, according to demand or opportunity." His writing was similar. It embodied all the virtues of informality and all of the defects of repetition. His sentences were often as long as others' paragraphs; paragraphs occasionally ran for two or three pages. It was, as Sontag wrote of Walter Benjamin, "as if each sentence [or paragraph, in Royce's case] had to say everything."

This intensely oral, rambling, and disputatious style may have begun as a reaction to his deprivation from such philosophical debate during his years as instructor at Berkeley. Although exciting, the Berkeley Club was general, diffuse, unprofessional. It was part of a society that he viewed much as he described the regents of the University of California, "a miscellaneous and comparatively ignorant body, . . . by fits and starts meddlesome, always stupid, not always friendly, and never competent or anxious to discover the nature of our work or of our ability." The West was not a society worth arguing with. He cherished in his own writing the kind of intellectual debate he missed as a young man.

His prose was rugged, untamed, untailored, far from the disciplined cadences of a Jefferson or an Emerson. Yet one modern philosopher feels that Royce's "apparently effortless flow of lucid exposition has a special sort of ponderous grace." He could reach mountain heights, prompting Vincent Buranelli, the Princeton critic, to overstate the case: "Royce is not an artist incapable of declining into inferior prose. He is an artist capable of rising into great prose." Two examples:

> These vast social forces [powers of industry, aggregations of capital] are like the forces of nature. They excite our loyalty as little as do the trade-winds or the blizzard. They leave our patriotic sentiments cold. The smoke of our civilization hides the very heavens that used to be so near, and the stars to which we were once loyal.

> But in our actual social life,—in the market-place, or at the political gathering, or when mobs rage and imagine a vain thing, in the streets of a modern city, the close shut-in streams of consciousness . . . seem to flow together like rivers that are lost in the ocean, and to surge into tumultuous unity, as if they were universal tides.

But between the peaks came the long desert stretches, the unshorn thickets of verbiage. His mother-in-law, at the end of a verbose letter to her daughter, added, "I'm worse than Royce who never knows when to stop." Always his compulsion to explain and convince overwhelmed his expressed, almost pitiful, desire for conciseness. Shortly before he died, he wrote the editor of the *Encyclopaedia of Religion and Ethics*, "As for my diffuseness, and intolerable long-windedness, you may cure that . . . with the aid of your waste basket." Once, after writing a nine-line sentence on the Self and wishing "to state the case more briefly," he digested the nine lines—and the result came out eight.

The ways in which Royce's arguments might reflect his West are not easy to discern, but they are there. Take, for example, his insistence on the primacy of the will. The first course he ever taught—to his fellows at Johns Hopkins—was on Schopenhauer, the "phantom ship" philosopher, whose sense of the human will led him to a tragic pessimism. Royce took the will, but not the pessimism. He saw reality itself as that which fulfills the purpose of an individual will. People are free, not determined; therefore, "to learn your own will,—yes, to create your own will, is one of the largest of your human undertakings." Those wills conflict in society, where human beings exhibit their instinctual desire to fight, their "elemental passion for conflict." Yet paradoxically those wills in friction could eventually produce a better society. In such a way Royce saw the western experience as a slow progression from the uncontrolled willfulness of hardhanded individuals, like cattlemen or miners, to the social controls provided by churches and governments. He saw California history in the same light. It was a dialectic in which the thesis of a tranquil society was disrupted by an antithesis of disorder (conquest, gold rush, vigilance committees, warfare against foreigners, and other "moral insanities"). The synthesis came with an awakening of conscience and the attainment of social order.

An emphasis on the will was a staple of nineteenth-century philosophy. Immanuel Kant, for one, laid its foundations, William James shared it, and Friedrich Nietzsche enlarged upon it. So the West can hardly be called its fount. Yet, other philosophers like Santayana were less concerned with the concept, and as Royce's usage of it in his history of California suggested, his background provided at least a predisposition toward the idea. The West did not cause Royce's emphasis on the will, but the two were congenial to one another.

If the will was important, so, too, must be the individual, its instrument. The individual is precious—"this stray wanderer from the animal kingdom, with his great brain and his aching heart, whose fantasies are his own worried soul seen in a dream." Royce shared with Alexis de Tocqueville an anxiety over social leveling in America with its "tendency to crush the individual." In Tocquevillian fashion he gave "every individual his unique place in the world order—his deed that nobody else can do, his will which is his own." The individual was significantly and morally free. This was sound eighteenth-century liberalism, to which Easterners might happily nod but for which Westerners would respond with a whoop and a holler. It is not surprising that, as we will see, Frederick Jackson Turner's frontier thesis was influenced by Royce.

This lifelong concern over the relation betweeen the individual and his or her society was given abundant room for exploration in Royce's *California*. "Every man looked out for himself in those days," he wrote about the mining camps, voicing his refrain on the kind of individualism that proved so destructive to society. Given the stress on that kind of individuality, how could one hope for community in the frontier setting? The philosophical problem would flower for Royce at the turn of the century in his *World and the Individual*. In that work as well as in *California*, the universal came first, and ultimately the individual must return to the realization that he or she is grounded in the universal, in the one reality. For example, Royce saw the mining camps composed of atomized individuals at the child's stage of milk and mother; they must someday grope for social cohesion.

But Royce, like John Locke, had a psychology to undergird his theory. We do not start with ourselves and then branch out to society. We know ourselves only through comparison and interpretations of others. The individual's purpose can be satisfied only by the other; it pivots around the ideas of his or her fellows, "of their esteem or rivalry, of the tasks that they set me to do, of my office as their comrade, opponent, rival, enemy, friend, or servant." The individual has no reality, no identity, until it acts in society.

In his mature philosophy, and especially in *The Problem of Christianity*, Royce saw more clearly how dual relationships, the dyads, are never sufficient; a third, mediating function is required. Without that element the two are what he called "dangerous pairs," opposed in their interests, the success of one leading to the failure of the other. In the triad they become "a community of interpretation." John Smith, the philosopher, has seen this idea in terms of Royce's essentially religious orientation: "Christianity has made possible that redeeming community without which the twin evils of individualism and collectivism cannot be overcome."

It is the community that tames the pride, directs the waywardness, and channels the restlessness of the individual. Royce saw the community as an ordered body of loyal individuals bound together by a remembered past (a community of memory) and a unifying future (a community of hope). Through this community, individuals, far from being lost, will be saved both in their individuality and from their individuality. Loyalty and community in turn will shield our society from the opposing evils of solipsism and collectivism.

Here, as in the doctrine of the will, it is easy to push connections too far. The concept of community was widespread in Royce's day. Raymond Jackson Wilson has shown convincingly that most late-nineteenth-century American thought was an effort to redirect the assumption that society was a barrier to the expressiveness of the individual; in other words, to assert the import of the community. Charles Sanders Peirce, John Dewey, Lester Frank Ward, E. A. Ross, and George Herbert Mead, were only a few of those demonstrating that society was a vital, functioning element in the growth of the individual. Jean Quandt has singled out nine others, including William Allen White, Jane Addams, and Charles Horton Cooley. Royce was squarely in the midst of this concern. Indeed, the later honing of his ideas came from his contacts with the old-line New Englander Peirce, and though several of these thinkers were influenced by Royce, none of them was raised in a gold-rush town.

Royce specifically claimed that his concept of community was rooted in his western experience. Coming as he did from a marginal fringe of the nation, it is perhaps natural that he better understood the local community as an avenue to the universal. Turner recognized national dimensions through his Middle West; Royce, from California. Neither of these regions was a center of power, but they may have come closer to producing essentially American traits than did Washington or New York. "If you want a great people to be strong, you must depend upon provincial loyalties to mediate between the people and their nation." Through local attachments diversity could embrace unity, and California in Royce's mind could prefigure the nation.

The mechanism through which the individual is bound to the community is *loyalty*, a key word in Royce's philosophy. "The only possible ethical use of an individual is to be loyal. He has no other destiny." Loyalty may be to family, to country, to religion, or to a cause, but in it individuals must lose themselves: "the willing, the thoroughgoing, and the practical devotion of a self to a cause," even, or most especially, to a lost cause. John Clendenning feels that the later twentieth century would use the word "commitment" to denote what Royce meant by "loyalty." Loyalty or commitment, Royce distinguished the idea from slavish subservience by requiring that it also include a loyalty to loyalty, which means that the cause must never be one that lessens the loyalty of others. The good of all must predominate, and any aggression on the rights of others is not in the service of loyalty. "Loyalty demands many members, but one body; many gifts, but one spirit." In an age that worried about the divisiveness of individualism, it is not surprising that Royce's *Philosophy of Loyalty* became the most popular and widely read of his books.

Royce's arguments on loyalty, not fully developed until 1908, were nevertheless germinated in a western context. His

experiences amid the strains and needs of an emerging incho-
ate western society gave plenty of room for such a theory.
How weak in Grass Valley were the third elements, larger than
the individual, to which one could be loyal. Government was
embryonic; Grass Valley did not even have an incorporated
city council until the year Josie was born. State laws, as for
example against gambling, were unenforceable. A common
society was hard to find. The itinerant mining class and the
more established businessmen (only a fraction of the population) lived in worlds apart. Heavy overtones of racism partially
explained the chasm. Such bifurcation was similar to that in
the state at large, for which Royce blamed Frémont and his
unnecessary militarization. Likewise, Royce's analysis of the
Sacramento squatter claims posed a split society. On all sides
was a population searching for ties of loyalty, and his mother
and their small, migrant group of churchgoers stood like a
lighthouse of loyalties in that nonloyal land.

If we seek to go beyond these indirect connections, we
might ask if in Royce's unexpressed assumptions there may be
found remnants of his western experience. He was, for example, a traditional conservative, a Burkean whose ideal was
homogeneous, organic wholeness. His loyalty to loyalty was a
conservative ethical ideal embracing traditional moral values.
Take his analysis of the problems of American society in
1908—dislocations caused by population growth, immigration, and consequent ethnic diversity; a war spirit that took
delight "in great armies and great navies for their own sake";
an overemphasis on prosperity, personal success, and national
greatness; declining family ties; the splintering caused by mutually hostile political parties, sects, and social classes, including corporate managers and organized labor; and a centralized
nationalism unsupported by provincial loyalties.

The common denominator in this list was divisiveness, a
further expression of those dyadic relationships, or "dangerous pairs," without third, mediating elements. He assumed
that an earlier society, the *Gemeinschaft*, decentralized but
unified, was superior because it demanded loyalty to a unit

larger than the self. Social rebellion (unlike intellectual icono-
clasm) was not an answer for Royce, as it was for Westerners
such as Ignatius Donnelly or Big Bill Haywood. Royce genuinely worried about the "restless spirit of our reforming age,"
yet he did not see rebellion as wholly evil. For Royce nothing
finite could be wholly good or evil, because it embodied a part
but yet not the whole of truth. A measure of rebelliousness
was thus good in that it allowed assertion in a cause, but it
was evil by not encompassing the good of obedience. One
may criticize a society, disapprove, and object: "Dissatisfied
with what now is, I press on towards what is yet to come."
But the assumption is that one should not "press on" as a social radical.

Royce's conservative premise may be compared with his
West's own ambiguous history of conservatism. If conservatism rests on tradition and social stability and prefers gradual-
ism over sudden change, the West certainly exhibited such in
its attention to schools and churches, its farm women dreaming of past security, its commitment to entrepreneurial and
corporate capitalism, and its vigilantes protecting the status
quo. Western radicalism was less obvious, though it was there—
women demanding the vote and educational equality, Populists proposing government ownership, socialists building com-
munitarian experiments, Wobblies singing of one big union.
The mining community produced both Josiah Royce and Big
Bill Haywood; California nurtured both Josiah Royce and
Henry George. But in the end, with a few exceptions as in
Ludlow, Colorado, or in the Populist Revolt, the thrust of the
West moved with Royce. The conservation of past values was
the proper course for rational and loyal beings.

One avenue in uncovering such assumptions is through
word choice. Let us take three words from Royce's works,
words he used so frequently that they of necessity reflect the
deeper currents of his mind—*practicality, wander,* and *sunder.*
"Practicality" exhibited Royce's pragmatic concern for action;
"wander," through the screen of his romantic sensibility, re-

flected frontier mobility; "sunder" underscored the need for unity in a pluralistic culture.

"That all theories have a practical meaning, I do indeed explicitly teach. That . . . is my whole philosophy." Loyalty to loyalty must become a "practical working scheme of life" by being made personal, simple, clear, concrete, effective, and teachable. The beauty of Paul's "beloved community" was that it had "a practical concreteness, a clear common sense about it." "Ideas are like tools. They are there for an end." And they must be "stained with the blood of the battlefields of real life."

For Royce, practicality went hand in hand with the empirical search for truth. Empiricism, a crusty denial of dogmatism and authority, was, like his pragmatism, an ideological equivalent of practicality. Jacques Barzun has seen such pragmatism as growing from "practicality, the individual, the pioneer optimism of those who by geographical good fortune see the road indefinitely open before them." With gusto Royce, the young pioneer, knew the down-to-earth practicality of the western environment, the hardheaded farmers and miners of a society that distrusted theory.

This is not to say that Royce's theme of practicality did not also grow from eastern, or broadly American, roots. His attachment to the philosophical equivalent of practicality, pragmatism, was the product of his association with men like Charles Sanders Peirce in Baltimore and Cambridge. Peirce, the founder of American pragmatism, claimed that Royce's *World and the Individual* came closer to pragmatism than anything the so-called pragmatists had written. Royce certainly believed that, first, truth would and should work or satisfy our need to know and that, second, human ideas and ethics were relative and subject to constant interpretation. Truth can never be grasped completely: "The realm of the empirical is always . . . fragmentary. But then this is the only realm known to men." "The question always is, Can the player win his chosen game, the artist succeed in his own selected art, the practical man accomplish his own task, and not the task of some other man?" This personalized truth is perceived through action, not abstraction. Knowing is acting: "My theoretical life is also practical." A community behaves like an entity; therefore it is a "working hypothesis" that it lives with a mind of its own.

Royce's pragmatism enveloped his pluralism with monism. Larger unities encompass the smaller in syntheses that end only with an Absolute. As he said of community, "Unless it is both one and many, it is no community at all." Unwilling to abandon the central pragmatic ideas yet unwilling to accept them without modification, he adopted for his philosophy an alternate and enigmatic term, "absolute pragmatism." As James said to a fellow pragmatist, Royce "swallows you whole without a cough or hiccup, simply insisting that the Absolute surrounds you." Then came a note of uncharacteristic Jamesian disparagement: "Royce, whenever he deals with details, works in good empiricist, pluralist fashion—his Absolute is only a surplus ornament which suits his humor."

That "humor," the pragmatist qua absolutist, the practical unified, might be seen as a philosophical expression of the tales he heard from his mother—struggling across the plains in 1849 with husband and baby, no others; seeing God in the burning sagebrush; and later memorializing her religious devotion to enlighten her son's historical study. In his histories he reflected her fear of the unstructured society stripping away the old certainties. Philosophically he was too much the iconoclast to follow her dogmatism. His lifelong search, however, for the truth of religion (beyond its usefulness) and his desire for a rationally and philosophically sound explanation of the Absolute were expressions of a pioneer woman and a chronic western search for order and certainty in the face of centrifugal social pluralism.

Royce's fundamental but unorthodox religious stance was not unlike the general history of religion in the West. In his *California* he saw religion as a keystone. Through the eyes of his mother even gold-rush San Francisco included "a very goodly array of pioneer churches, supported by active and not

poverty-stricken societies." Religion was not just social cement; it was society's affirmation of the universal, the door
through which individuals could exercise expressive differences while conforming to the unity of tradition.

The philosopher shared much with missionaries such as
Marcus and Narcissa Whitman or with Jean Pierre DeSmet,
wrestling with the hard practicalities of forest and kitchen
while holding firmly to spiritual values beyond experience.
The missionary mind, of course, derided the experiential dimension as lesser, something to be vanquished, hardly a legiti-
mate test of truth, and in this respect Royce did not follow it.

Perhaps Royce's practical bent stood him closer to a Westerner like John Muir, who moved beyond a fundamentalist
background and an early courtship with engineering into a
message about the transcendent spirit of the wilderness. Royce
and Muir were both comfortable with pioneer pragmatism,
but, like Albert Bierstadt painting a western mountain, they
wrapped it in a spiritual glow. And both Royce and Muir gave
particular meaning to Turner's paradoxical combination of
idealism with materialism as one trait in the western character.

Another clue to Royce's assumptions, in this case his essential romanticism, lies in his use of the word "wander." "For
Royce," said Michael Weinstein, "human beings are essentially
wanderers whose deepest doubt is about their proper destination." "So I have indeed tried," wrote Royce, "to speak as one
wanderer speaks to another who is his friend, when the way is
long and obscure." He never tired of quoting from John Bunyan's *Pilgrim's Progress*, a favorite from his childhood. Wandering lay deep in his family tradition. His father was steeped in
a restlessness that would have done justice to a Hawkeye, a
Huck Finn, or a Childe Harold, and the West from which
Royce sprang was a land of roamers. Remember that in 1856
only five persons in Grass Valley remained out of every one
hundred who had been there five years before. "Wander" suggests all the related words and metaphors so frequent in his
prose: restlessness, search, quest, pilgrimage, road, and home.
John Clendenning finds these words of psychological signifi-

cance, inhabiting his mind like ghosts of his father, the root-less fruit vendor.

As undeniable as Clendenning's insight may be, it is also true that wandering is a romantic idea, and Royce was temperamentally attuned with the romantics. His love for romantic music and poetry resonated with poets he knew such as T. S. Eliot and e. e. cummings. Bliss Carman, the vagabond poet, in 1891 revealed that Royce's *Religious Aspect of Philosophy* was "a very constant old friend, with its gusts of poetry all through the pages. I have journeyed with it in my canoe, and delighted in it enough to be a much more sensible person than I am."

Royce's philosophy was sprinkled with poetic references and quotations (some thirty-seven in his most erudite work, *The World and the Individual*, and over twenty in *The Problem of Christianity*). The largest number of these quotations came from Shakespeare, not strictly speaking a romantic, but the next in order were Goethe, Tennyson, Browning, Omar Khayyam, Wordsworth, Byron, Shelley, Goldsmith, and Gray. As with "wander" Royce loved romantic words like "caprice," which he used in all of his books and eight times in the second volume of *The World and the Individual* alone. No single category of his metaphors is more abundant than those dealing with nature: growth, flowers, trees, forests, birds and animals, lakes and streams, storms and seasons, wind and sea, earth and sky, sun and stars.

Yet this romantic idea is not an ethical goal. He was not an Emerson for whom nature led the individual to the Oversoul while society was generally a barrier. For Royce, not by wandering abroad, nor through an inner awakening or a transcendent experience with nature, but by imitating others in the society is the self realized. The child begins with an undifferentiated, universal world, and only slowly recognizes individual elements like mother and milk. Wandering subsides, overtaken in time by imitation, attachment, and finally loyalty (or commitment), producing individuality. Individuals might profitably begin with wandering, but they must ultimately find themselves in its cessation.

Loyal individuals, still basically "proud, untamed, restless, insatiable in our private self-will," are always free to betray their commitment and resume their wandering, becoming footloose Westerners, like Royce's father, drifting from mining camp to mining camp. That betrayal, however, is the supreme evil, the deed for which individuals can never thereafter forgive themselves. It "has reduced to its primal chaos the fair order of those who trusted and who lived and loved together in one spirit!" and it "rends asunder what love has joined in dear unity."

Another word that Royce seemed to love was "sunder". He chose it twenty-eight times in *The Problem of Christianity* and sixty-eight times in *The World and the Individual*. In one nine-page section he averaged one use of it per page and elsewhere on a single page elected it six times. Associated with his frequent metaphor of the chasm, the connotations of "sunder" in the short run were unhappy—shatter, fragment, break, rend, strip of meaning, create barriers; seldom are there implications of freedom, release, or birth.

Sundering, however, is an essential part of the temporal human condition, and Royce used the idea to prove the existence of third levels of consciousness. "For otherwise the sundering would exist without being fully and consciously present to anybody; since, insofar as a is sundered from b, there is, neither in a alone nor in b alone, a consciousness of all that the sundering implies for both." Differences always involve likenesses. From one viewpoint, two books are different in being red and blue; from another, they are alike in sharing the concept of color. In a similar way, sundering becomes part of a dialectical process leading to increasing levels of understanding and unity.

Ultimately an idea or object cannot be sundered from the larger network. "The whole of this world stands or falls together." "I know that I have no Being whatever which can be sundered from the Being of my fellow man." Loyalty to the community, once again, is the mechanism by which sundered human beings are joined; here in "his ideally extended self" the individual finds "the unity, the wealth, and the harmony of plan which his sundered natural existence never supplies."

The idealistic problem was to show how even this sundered world revealed unity, like Black Elk, the Sioux, picturing a hoop that surrounds the world of experience. Unlike the Indian, however, Royce in his solution invoked science, especially evolution. The beauty of all the sciences is not their quantitative analyses but their exact form of serial order. "Not Quantity, but Order, is the fundamental category of exact thought about facts." Because science is so involved in placing facts in series—in chemistry, in physics, in geology, and especially in the whole Darwinian enterprise, it constantly reinforces the ways in which a third element binds together temporally sundered objects. Unity might then triumph over shattered chaos, not through revelation, but through the logical workings of science.

None of these words was peculiarly western (not "hard-nosed," "mosey," or "bust"), but they bore the unexpressed connotations of Royce's life and experience, and their meanings and implications were embedded in the western tradition. "Practicality" was action not thought, and action was what the young Royce found enthroned over intellect in the West. He wrote of vigilantes justifying their violence in practical terms. He understood how mining-camp government emerged from practicalities like the protection of claims and gold dust. He was reared in a society of frontierpeople "quick to find expedients," and "wandering" suggests the extreme mobility into which he was born. Never blind to romantic unrealities, he distrusted the romanticism of Bret Harte. But he clearly recognized more realistic restlessness in the rampant fevers of land speculation by frontierpeople like the Scotch-Irish or Daniel Boone. He observed how a wandering population used its manifest destiny to extol decentralization while at the same time it cried for federal legislation. "Sunder" could also describe cultural conflict in Royce's pluralistic mining West— ethnic groups such as the Mexicans driven into social banditry, Indians displaced from their land, Chinese excluded from certain occupations. Royce realized how the selfish disdain for authority bred lawlessness. He experienced the economic isolation of the West before the transcontinental telegraph and railroad. He witnessed the fears and doubts of fractured frontier society as well as the vaulting individualism that, as with a Paul Bunyan, left human beings dominating nature yet spiritually divorced from it. Here was, indeed, a practical, wandering, sundered society that Royce knew and projected, and every one of these themes was close to Royce in his own western experience or carefully described by him in his historical writing.

The West continued to play a part, not in Royce's historical work alone, but through the words, the metaphors, the hidden meaning of content and context that infused his entire philosophical corpus. Through Josiah Royce California and the mining frontier thus crept, as his beloved Browning might have put it, like "a soft star trembles through the drifting clouds" into America's golden age of philosophy.

CHAPTER II

Retrospect

The frontiersman may wander; but he must some day win what shall belong to the united empire of human truth. Those are wrong who ask him merely to stay at home. He wanders because he must; and God is to be found also in the wildernesses and in the solitary places of thought. But those are right who ask that the student of philosophy shall find, if he succeeds at all, a living truth; and that the God of the wilderness, if indeed he be the true God, shall show himself also as the keeper of the city.

Royce, *World and the Individual*

"I am now an oldish professor, who stoops a little, and carries too many books about, and plans many books that I do not write. I am already supposed by younger colleagues to be an old fogey." In 1908 Royce's judgment on his aging was certainly premature. At the same time he fretted that William James, his senior, absorbed "all the interest on his side" while Royce passed into an early professional obscurity. There, too, he may have been hasty, for seven years later in 1915 at the age of sixty he received a rousing tribute of a kind not yet given to James, indeed seldom accorded to living scholars.

It was Philadelphia just after Christmas. In an unprecedented move, the American Philosophical Association devoted two of its formal sessions to Josiah Royce and his work, and then honored him in a glittering dinner at the Walton Hotel (later the John Bartram, site of the present Hershey Hotel). On Broad Street at the corner of Locust, the imposing site of Royce's triumph was ten stories with mansard roof, Flemish gables, and turrets at the corners, "leaking golden flame at every window against the green azure of the dusk." The dining room shone in the style of Louis XVI, and the dinner was grand from the oysters to the mince pie. Philosophers from Harvard, Yale, Princeton, Columbia, Michigan, Pennsylvania, and California extolled Royce; and John Dewey, A. O. Lovejoy, Bertrand Russell, Henri Bergson, and a host of others sent congratulatory messages to be read. They responded to those thirty-four years during which Royce represented the first and greatest department of philosophy that Harvard or any other American university has ever known. He remained in his colleagues' eyes something between a Rubens and a John L. Sullivan of philosophy.

When he arose after dinner to accept the plaudits of his peers, his talk began with a remarkable return to his Grass Valley childhood in the Far West, to the "mining town in the Sierra Nevada," only a bit older than himself. He recalled "a very frequent wonder as to what my elders meant when they said that this was a new community." To a boy, he said, the rotting cabins and miners' graves looked old. He remembered also the wonder of the sunsets over Avon Farm, his enjoyment of Bible stories while he rebelled against Bible school, his delight in arguments with his sisters, his school days in San Francisco where the first blows from the rough and tumble life of other boys taught him "the majesty of the community." In reviewing his frontier life, he came now to see "that my deepest motives and problems have centred about the Idea of the Community" and "by what I nowadays try to express by teaching that we are saved through the community." The speech was an extraordinary climax to his life and a rare glimpse into the effects of a western childhood on an intellectual career.

Royce lived for only one more year, a period overshadowed by the storm clouds of World War I. In those months Germany, Royce's beloved Germany—the land of Schopenhauer and Hegel and Beethoven now twisted by Kaiser Wilhelm— sharpened its military might and loosed it on targets like the *Lusitania* and eventually on Belgium. The blows descended on Josiah like crimes against his own person. He fell into both rage and heartache. Years later, Thomas Mann reacted the same way about another generation's Germany, "clung round by demons, a hand over one eye, with the other staring into horrors, down she flings from despair to despair."

Never content with despair, Royce summoned his remaining strength for the fight. As a boy of eight in "Pussy Blackie's Travels," he asked what soldiers are good for. Now he knew. In tones of the Old Testament's Josiah, he called for war against his spiritual homeland and, though tired and old, gave speech after speech recalling the mark of Cain and the treason of Judas. "In the flames and burning periods of denunciation," he spent his final fury. A spectator at one of those meetings described the pitch of enthusiasm, the salvos of prolonged applause, Royce's "deep undertone of moral indignation." "It was the heartening spectacle of a great man first rousing and then voicing the collective will of a perplexed community."

His own philosophy stood close by to sustain him. Evil, often but part and parcel of the evolving good, might in the form of the coming struggle sprout some hope for global community. If Germany committed the extreme of treason in a betrayal of human society, its chastened return would strengthen all parties, for it required the creation of a third, mitigating participant to whom they could all be loyal. The message was published as *The Hope of the Great Community*, his final statement to the world, his final vision.

In the spring of 1916, Horace Kallen, student and disciple of his cultural pluralism, happened upon Royce in Harvard Yard. "His steps seemed hesitant and unnaturally short. . . . When I greeted him, his round blue eyes looked staring, and without recognition. And then he said in a voice somehow thinner, . . . 'You are on the side of humanity, aren't you?'"

For the final time he refused President Benjamin Ide Wheeler's repeated offer of the Mills Professorship of Philosophy at the University of California. It was his last chance to return to his roots in the West. His student William Ernest Hocking once wrote Royce (in gratitude for the Indian book Royce sent to Hocking's son Richard) that California "is a place of courage rather than of comfort, and there is a time for each of these." California was once his youthful source of courage; it could never be for him a sanctuary of comfort.

In August he fell seriously ill, and on September 14, 1916, in his bed at 103 Irving Street, he died of a stroke brought on by arteriosclerosis. His beloved Goethe would have asked for him that he die and have new birth, rebirth in the communal memory of his followers; and Goethe might speak of that great engine of a brain no longer functioning on the darkened earth, Faust's bargain complete, and the details of time and place merged at last into eternity. John Bunyan's pilgrim Christian stood beyond the City of Destruction out of the reach of Giant Despair in the country of Beulah, where he felt the warm sun and heard the voice of the turtle in the land. And at the gates of the Heavenly City, the Beloved Community, he sang:

> Put by the curtains, look within my veil,
> Turn up my metaphors, and do not fail,
> There, if thou seekest them, such things to find,
> As will be helpful to an honest mind.

On that same September day Royce's admirer Woodrow Wilson campaigned for a second term as president of the United States, and less noted, Colonel John T. Thompson was setting up his company to promote a lightweight, multiple-round, submachine gun to be known by armies of soldiers, strikebreakers, and gangsters as the tommy gun. Wilson himself died fighting for the League of Nations, a form of Royce's great community, but the tommy gun and its successors helped make the Wilson-Roycean dream a chimera. In the Second Book of Kings the Lord spoke at last to King Josiah, "Because thine heart was tender, . . . thou shalt be gathered into thy grave in peace; and thine eyes shall not see all the evil which I will bring upon this place."

Royce's passing was marked everywhere in the eastern academic world, and none the less in the American West. The *Fresno Republican* called him affectionately "our California philosopher." A few hundred miles south a representative memorial service at Pomona College judged that Royce knew more science than the average scientist, more literature than the literary scholar, and held "a far deeper insight into philosophic truths than any other modern thinker." In sparsely settled, rough-and-ready Montana, the *Anaconda Standard* reviewed Royce's writings and predicted his future "rank as an American genius." Four days after his death, the Berkeley student paper, the *Daily Californian*, printed a long obituary praising Royce as "California's most noted alumnus" and proclaiming his death a bitter blow to America and humanity.

Outside the circles of historical philosophy, as pragmatism, relativism, and positivism came to dominate American thought, the memory of Josiah Royce noticeably faded. On the other hand, as late as World War II a liberty ship the *Josiah Royce* sailed in another battle against German militarism. And, more lasting, a striking western building commemorates his name, just as Emerson Hall at Harvard honors the Sage of Concord. Ten years after Royce's death, when a branch campus of the University of California moved from temporary quarters in Los Angeles to a new site west of the city, its central auditorium and classroom building was christened Royce Hall and became UCLA's "best-loved and best-known structure." The imposing Romanesque towers and porticoes faced with brick as red as the hair of his youth stand today as Royce's enduring memorial. Over its proscenium the architect carved a maxim that would have aroused in Royce a prolonged tirade: "Education is learning to use the tools which the race has found indispensable." These words came from the first provost, Ernest Carroll Moore, who revered Royce but unwittingly expressed a utilitarian sentiment far closer to William James. Over a front portal, however, leading to the classroom corridor, in everlasting stone and opposite a quotation from Plato, was chiseled a pure Roycean phrase: "The world is a progressively realized community of interpretation."

This book sees Royce largely in terms of his western American implications, his relevance to the section that bore him. It

Royce Hall, UCLA. The most enduring physical memorial to Josiah Royce, completed in 1929. The proposal that UCLA's central building be named for the philosopher came from his former student Charles Rieber, the Dean of the new College of Letters and Science. Those in charge thought first to name the library for Royce, but on consideration the chief classroom and lecture hall was felt more likely to preserve his name. (Courtesy University of California, Los Angeles)

is fair, finally, to ask not only to what extent he was indeed a Westerner but also what is here meant by the West, what exerted this continuing, subtle influence. To begin with, it must be remembered that there obviously was no single West, no single frontier, no single western mind. Royce's life, like any other, could not represent *the* West. His boyhood experiences, however, were one West, one frontier, one category of frontier thought. Many people on the frontier never felt intellectually at home in the West. Like the elder Shimerda in Willa Cather's *My Antonia*, they played their violins alone in an alien environment. Many consequently transplanted themselves eastward, and because in young manhood Royce also did so, his approach to the West was one of transference. His subsequent commentaries on California, notably his history and his novel, were expressed from an eastern chair, as with Mark Twain or the later Bernard DeVoto. His life was not the cohering model of a Walter Prescott Webb, a Charles Howard Shinn, or a Wallace Stegner. Nor was his the kind of reference model of born-Easterners such as Owen Wister or Frederic Remington, who partook of the West, only to return to the East for the platform of their observations. Neither coherence nor reference, Royce's transference model made of him a western intellectual who on the physical edge of the continent took a logical route to the East, carrying a metaphysical sense of the West to the intellectual capital of the nation.

Combining the two stock models of the American, the Puritan and the pioneer, Royce was both a product of and a reaction against his West. He transcended the West, grew beyond its confines, just as he came to celebrate a philosophy that embraced individual and provincial humanity in an enlarged common community. But he could more easily surpass his West because he was a Westerner, because he represented the independence that he felt was the birthright of a Californian.

One could find that birthright descending less from California than from his mother, the essential Easterner; whatever he brought from his western experience was in the end dwarfed by what he acquired maternally. That "truly pious among these struggling wanderers," fighting the forces of disorder, instilled in Royce an evangelical conviction that society could and should be reformed through moral means. Stephen Royce thought that Josiah's reluctance "to march with the crowd" stemmed from Sarah Royce's devotion to the old ideals. "The raw new country," he wrote, "the wild and even lawless character of many of its inhabitants, found no reflection, no faintest yielding, in the stern standards of his mother." But this is not to say that either Josiah or Sarah were therefore less western. In the process of following her restless husband (the man who never prospered but at least persisted), Sarah transmuted her eastern self into a western woman. A devotion, even obsession, with past values was a firm plank in the mindset of many pioneer women. Royce's frontier rearing was just as representative as that of Hamlin Garland or John Muir in other western regions.

A conservative intellectual like Royce is presumed to be at odds with the progressive activist go-ahead western environment. Royce was certainly a practical worker, but he may have felt some uneasiness, some embarrassment at being a conservative intellectual and a Westerner at the same time. He once wrote his friend Alfred Deakin in Australia, "Being a lonely and abstract student, I have no sort of return to offer you, who are an empire-builder, and a man of affairs." Royce was not an empire builder in any sense, even in philosophy. But he did not damn the West in which he was born. He did not see it as conservative thinkers such as Frances Trollope or Frederick Marryat saw it, as a land of decadence and brutality, the natural product of a libertarian heritage. Instead he championed his West as an exhibition of the strengths (and also weaknesses) of individualism. At the same time he reserved the right to be its archfoe and point out its evasion of community. His California contemporary Jack London revealed a divided allegiance between stark individualism (*The Call of the Wild*) and romantic socialism (*The Iron Heel*), and hence, with little else in common, he reflected some of Royce's ambiguity between the conservative intellectual and the liberal activist.

It is fruitful to conjecture what might have happened to Royce if William James had not summoned him to Harvard in the spring of 1882. He would almost certainly not have become as great a philosopher, and the West would count another flower born to blush unseen. Perhaps he would instead have become a more direct spokesman for the relevance of the western experience to the East, in the manner of the St. Louis Hegelians or historians such as Merle Curti or Vernon Louis Parrington. A greater danger would have been the loss of a grandness of vision, as happened with Charles Shinn. He shared with Royce a rural California boyhood, education at the newborn University of California, graduate study at Johns Hopkins, and an early perception of California caught up in the sweep of Anglo-American culture. But Shinn returned to California to stay, abandoned history to work for the Forest Service, and lost his broader dream. It may have been fortunate for the history of the West that Royce was called East.

Nevertheless, sometimes directly, more often inadvertently, Royce became a spokesman for the West. Indeed for Bernard DeVoto, another western interpreter sitting in a Cambridge chair, Royce's *California* was "the study that remains for the whole the best one." More recently Patricia Nelson Limerick called Royce the "father of Western history." Her comment is particularly interesting because Limerick in her work finds the frontier not at an end but part of a long history of conquest that preceded and succeeded it. Royce would approve, for to him historical compartmentalizing like ending the frontier in 1890 would be puzzling. The frontier did not make Americans special or unique; they were still part of the human race. The western story was not free land, demographic statistics, or census lines. It was an internalization of the economic and social factors, an eternal dialogue between the individual and the community. "The works of creation are glorious because they are in eternal movement and action." The frontier with all its conflict is ongoing. On a metaphoric level Michael Weinstein makes the same point: "Using Royce's imagery, the wilderness surrounds the city on all its sides and will always do so, however far the city pushes out."

In western American historiography Royce holds a pivotal place, coming as he did after Parkman, coincidental with Bancroft, and before Turner. One critic would place Royce's *California* close on the shelf with Parkman's *Oregon Trail* and Prescott's *Conquest of Mexico*. There is no evidence that Royce ever read Parkman or Prescott, but he wrote in their tradition of preprofessional history (not academically trained or in the academy). Bancroft and Royce were professionals with sources, even engaging in sophisticated oral history. But Royce added an extra measure of literary allusion and an even greater dose of philosophy. He deduced a momentous moral from a short compass and dealt with only one decade. Bancroft conversely drew little morality from an enormous canvas covering millennia. In this respect Royce was more the intellectual, dissecting and analyzing, while Bancroft was the scholar, the judge pronouncing balanced appraisals of the documentary evidence. Bancroft stood more in a tradition that would produce Reuben Gold Thwaites and Henry Wagner. These men felt the frontier as significant and proved their belief by telling its story in glorious detail. Royce went on to raise the detail itself into grand moment, illuminating nothing less than a national and humanistic frame.

As the intellectual, Royce was more the precursor of Turner. Unlike Parkman or Bancroft, Royce and Turner were both academics, capable of detailed documentary appraisals, but both are remembered more for theory than detail. Turner made the frontier a deterministic force; the frontier prescribed the participatory nature of our democracy and our peculiar obsession with individualism. Such determinism was far less obvious in Royce, and what was there tended to be negative. The frontier, an irresponsible society broken by violence and special interests, blocked the natural progression to order; like life itself, it was "restless, capricious, and therefore tragic."

Only when individuals chose to exert their wills could the dialectic be set in motion to redirect that irresponsibility into stability, and that was possible only when individuals were engaged in a cause that transcended their selfishness. Turner's frontier contained all the force of gravity; Royce's frontier embodied all the dangers of a centrifuge.

Just as Royce relied on Bancroft, so Turner capitalized on Royce. Turner was intrigued with Royce's analysis of provincialism and quoted him on that subject in various lectures, in *The Frontier in American History*, and in *The Significance of Sections in American History*. He quoted Royce on conformity (a "remorseless mechanism—vast, irrational") and worried over the passions of the mob. And he found an antidote in "the promise of what that wise and lamented philosopher, Josiah Royce called, 'the beloved community.' In the spirit of the pioneer's 'house raising' lies the salvation of the Republic."

But Royce went beyond Turner in providing through his life's work what Daniel Boorstin called "a philosophical substitute for the frontier." Whereas earlier thinkers such as Emerson and Whitman asked Americans, especially those on the frontier, to be sufficient in themselves, Royce found self-reliance not enough; along with the individual, the state and the community were equally vital players. And the frontier could teach that point just as well as the city. In the frontier's school of hard knocks, in every barn raising, every miners' meeting, every exchange of work, the values of community thrived. The Puritans understood how the threats and temptations of the wilderness caused people to work for the common good, and so the frontier might lead to the highest self-fulfillment, might provide the best road to self-definition. In this respect, too, Royce was a Puritan disciple, turning the frontier into what John Owen King described as a landscape of revelation. The wilderness revealed the eternal moral struggle, in which the community offered the primary guidance for sorting out what to preserve from the past.

When Turner came to Harvard in 1910, Royce had already been there twenty-eight years. The two men sat beside one another at a dinner party one evening in 1912. Turner found Royce "very bright and interesting," especially since Royce was exulting that night over Woodrow Wilson's election, and Wilson was dear to Turner's heart. These two men, chatting over their soup and wine, each in his way saw far beyond the details of western history into "the twilight regions of our historical consciousness." That was a phrase that Royce wrote long before, about the time Turner conceived his famous essay on the frontier. Royce embarked on that twilight road almost a decade before Turner more dramatically lit the trail.

On one level Royce was far more than a western intellectual. He was indeed, as Woodrow Wilson said, "a walking, sentient mind, agog about everything," and that sort of mind transcends place. Seen in this way, his life was less a western quest than a more general heroic quest, the kind that Clifford Geertz describes as the departure from ancestral shores grown stultifying, the journey to a different world full of surprises, tests, and revelations, and finally a deepened knowledge of reality and an obligation to communicate to those left behind. One could say that Royce's life and his experience fit into a pattern as old as civilization.

But on another level, because he lived twenty-four of his first twenty-seven years in the West and continued to take those origins seriously, we must categorize Royce as a western intellectual. That type is not a familiar one in western historiography. Americans as a whole favor the Custers at a Little Big Horn or the Travises at an Alamo and downplay the western thinker. Readers have found little excitement in a boy who devotes himself to *Faust* at the age of thirteen.

Yet the West was hardly devoid of intellectuals. In the Midwest after the 1850s the group of St. Louis Hegelians, which Royce visited as a new Ph.D., pioneered American philosophy. William Torrey Harris, Henry Brokmeyer, and George H. Howison imported their transcendentalism and Hegelianism from New England and from Germany, but they deliberately migrated to the Mississippi to explore the meaning of life. They may have represented a minor pocket of thought, but they were not unique. If we restrict ourselves only to the generation of Josiah Royce, a sampling of western intellectuals would include not only Turner but Lincoln Steffens, Charles Shinn, Albert Michalson, John Muir, John R. Commons, and Richard Ely. A particularly interesting example was William Ernest Hocking, raised in Joliet, Illinois. Like Royce, he was the child of camp meetings and evangelism and as a young man turned from engineering to philosophy. Though he, too, ended at Harvard by way of California, Hocking frequently referred to his youth in "the briar-bush of the Midwest." The life of Charles Henry Rieber, another philosopher, was cut to a similar pattern. Rieber was born in Placerville, California, and graduated from Berkeley in 1888. When he went to Harvard to teach, his children were shunned as playmates because they were thought to be uncouth Westerners. Still to them at night he would ecstatically narrate his childhood on the California mining frontier. Royce, Hocking, Rieber, and all these intellectuals not only emerged from various parts of the West but their lives, just as readily as the trapper, the miner, the Indian, or the Hispanic, symbolized Limerick's "legacy of conquest." The conquered, subservient province along with its intellectuals sought interdependence and sometimes flight.

As an intellectual, did Royce see his West differently from others? Did he grasp any peculiar meanings for the West? Can the West be reinterpreted through the eyes of Josiah Royce? The answers to those questions have already been addressed or implied. They can be summarized here, however, using three of his major philosophical concepts: the individual, the community, and the province.

Royce, unlike James Fenimore Cooper, found the western loner something less than glorious. He wrote of "the brutal freedom of the pioneers—which I have found vile." Such a person can never be truly happy until he or she realizes the values of unity in a common cause, of interaction for the common good. Individuals in the West seldom respected the community; their image of it was often a Frankenstein vision, all elbows, shanks, and knees, the creature of human beings, not their source and nurture. As George Herbert Mead put it, "The communities came from him, not he from the community."

For Royce, in contrast, the community preceded the individual and symbolized the affirmation of belief and tradition in a collective person. The wilderness, however, expressed the absence of identity, even personal doubts about fundamental values. Thus California history—all western history—became "the struggle of society to impress the true dignity and majesty of its claims on wayward and blind individuals, and the struggle of the individual man, meanwhile, to escape, like a fool, from his moral obligations to society."

Once confirmed, that community becomes the source of a wise provincialism. The province can be as large as a region or as small as a family or an ethnic enclave, but it must have a sense of its own place, its own uniqueness, its own history, and its distinct future. Through its belief in decentralization, it upholds diversity and cultural pluralism. In the face of national impersonality, "Freedom, I should say, dwells now in the small social group, and has its securest home in provincial life. . . . The province must save the individual." The frontier was thus interpreted as both region and process—a region in which a wise provincialism might be practiced and a process in which individuals worked out their relations with the emerging community.

The process proceeded historically as a wavering dialectic. Nature was the thesis, humankind the antithesis, and the community the synthesis. The system faltered when people, like Royce's father, simply wandered. Then, though often obsessed with a dream of perfection (the ultimate gold strike, the grandest rendezvous, the final justification), the individual actually became the lonely miner or trapper, the uncommitted prostitute, the cranky pioneer—ineffectual, restless, burdened, wandering in the faceless wilderness. The process could halt again when the group (for example, the western town) stooped smugly to a narrow dogmatic provincialism and ceased to rise through wider provincialisms toward an absolute community. That town, even though it dreamed of churches, schools, railroads, and good women, in fact became the mean backwater with its irresponsible vigilantes, its self-centered speculators, its ethnic persecutors. California for a time became such a backwater, as did much of the West. Western development was a faltering process and went through a "dark night of the soul," which Royce (as James did later) might well have quoted from St. John of the Cross.

Has Royce's view of the West any significance to those who live nearly a century afterward? Certainly so, if we remember that Royce was one of the first to diagnose alienation, the American neurotic illness, the "inward revolt" of people who increasingly find it difficult to attach themselves to the community. The modern man, Royce said, quoting Jesus, wanders "in waste places and, when he returns, finds the lonely house of his individual life empty, swept, and garnished."

Our society has long recognized the disintegrating effects of modernization and the consequent need for community. From Nietzsche to Robert Bellah the crisis of individualism has been proclaimed. John Dewey, E. A. Ross, Lester Ward, Edward Bellamy, and Henry Adams, a few early voices, are echoed by Paul Tillich ("There is no life where there is no 'otherness'"), Martin Buber ("Where there is no sharing, there is no reality"), T. S. Eliot ("What life have you if you have not life together?"), Michael Lerner ("the pain generated by the absence of community"), James McBride Dabbs ("It is only by the handle of the community that we are able to pick up the world"), or the popular M. Scott Peck ("In and through community lies the salvation of the world"). The chorus sounds like Josiah Royce in an echo chamber, a candle in a hall of mirrors ("My life means nothing, either theoretically or practically, unless I am a member of a community").

For the malady the prescription from Dr. Royce is "conscience, duty, service," and an understanding of loyalty to loyalty by which people transmute their causes from a "war spirit" into genuine respect for the causes of others. But Royce went on. He clearly saw the dangers in mass conformity, in the "aimless crowd" as community. He understood how the cause might become militant enthusiasm, fanaticism, the insistent demand to impose one's loyalties on others, as in the early-twentieth-century antagonisms between labor and management, between rural and urban, or especially between more recent single-purpose political organizations. He did not show how to prevent conflict, nor did he wish to, but he did point the way to conducting conflict with respect and dignity. Without that consideration for the loyalty of others, people in their frustration turn to hedonistic indulgence, pure solipsism, or, perhaps more sympathetically, to plans for revision of the outward forms of community. Royce asked instead that we begin with the self and see the community as a "necessary condition of the emancipation of the self-conscious, self-directing individual." Royce was intent upon a sound individualism as well as a sound community. True, both can be distorted and exaggerated; but both can be corrected and restored. Loyalty to loyalty provides the tolerance of differences and, more important, respect for those differences; provincialism, with its profound sense of place, provides the necessary balance to social leveling.

Royce speaks to us, too, as a unifier, a historical synthesizer, a philosophical monist, and as such, he supports all the holistic strivings of modern humanity. To others, those who stand with the pluralism of William James, this is the terrifying part of Royce, suggesting the totalitarianism of our times. Royce, of course, would declare his philosophy to be the exact reverse: since the individual requires the community for self-knowledge and the truest community is a community of interpretation, Royce is defining the community as a process of communication that never contracts but enlarges humanity, hence can never be totalitarian. Or at least it is no more totalitarian than Puritanism, because the community, "a vast society of finite beings," is the ultimate expression of the individual.

It was the same way Royce looked on history. The chief trouble with the early annalists of San Francisco was their "mere rubbish-heap of broken facts. . . . They had no conception of the sense of it." He criticized Hubert Howe Bancroft for not bringing "unity of the many currents of the narrative into one great stream." His was the prophecy of synthesis, which emerged much later in the most recent "new history." Of course, Royce's consensus was nothing less than the heart of human experience, a reach so broad that it seems pontifical. As Morton White said, however, thinkers should not be persuaded "to avoid the search for a coherent view of such matters as history, law, politics, religion, or education by monitory analysts who cry: 'Remember Royce!'"

In the end we come down to Benedetto Croce's view that, even if not original, Royce was humanely wise. His was Tillich's ultimate concern. "I can be genuinely in love with the community only in case I have somehow fallen in love with the universe." Royce once said of a philosopher, "His immediate end may have been unattained; but thousands of years may not be long enough to develop for humanity the full significance of his reflective thought." Thereby he early and inadvertently wrote his own eulogy.

Josiah Royce loved his native California for what its story said about the American West and particularly about American values. Physically he left the West; intellectually he embraced its message throughout his life. It can be argued that Royce had to transcend California in order to become an intellectual, that he was in no sense a California philosopher but rather a German idealist, that his life represented an escape from the crudities of the frontier, and that all of his significant ideas germinated elsewhere. Such criticism is at best defining its terms narrowly. Any life is the amalgamation of the direction it faces and the experiences that intersect that bearing. California determined Royce's course; the rest was elaboration, though admittedly extensive. Greatness must intellectually outgrow the society in which it is born. Royce's birthplace gave him an experience with a very young, immature community, an exposure that he both focused and expanded in his life and work. Call him a frontiersman whose providence was to wear the purple robes of philosophy, and remember that in the year before he died, he came to think that the rest of his life was a resonance from his earliest beginnings. Josiah Royce was a philosopher who was "by destiny forever a frontiersman."

Bibliographical Note

The Papers of Josiah Royce (hereafter cited as RP) and of his immediate family, along with those of many of his friends and colleagues such as Charles Lanman and Ralph Barton Perry, are housed in the Harvard University Archives, Pusey Library, Harvard; while the William James Papers are upstairs in the Houghton. Other important collections used here are in the Bancroft Library, University of California, Berkeley (hereafter cited as BL), and a body of published work in Special Collections of the University of California, Los Angeles.

A detailed, annotated bibliography by Ignas Skrupskelis of Royce's works is in John J. McDermott, ed., *Basic Writings of Josiah Royce*, 2 vols. (Chicago: University of Chicago Press, 1969), and need not be repeated here. Equally indispensable was *The Letters of Josiah Royce*, ed. John Clendenning (Chicago: University of Chicago Press, 1970).

John Clendenning's *Life and Thought of Josiah Royce* (Madison: University of Wisconsin Press, 1985) is the definitive biography, to be placed beside Bruce Kuklick, *Josiah Royce: An Intellectual Biography* (Indianapolis: Bobbs-Merrill, 1972), and Frank M. Oppenheim, *Royce's Voyage Down Under: A Voyage of the Mind* (Lexington: University Press of Kentucky, 1980), and his *Royce's Mature Philosophy of Religion* (Notre Dame, Ind.: University of Notre Dame Press, 1987). Briefer treatments are Vincent Buranelli, *Josiah Royce* (New York: Twayne, 1964), and Thomas F. Powell, *Josiah Royce* (New York: Twayne, 1974). Some broader studies include extended discussions of Royce; the ones I have found most helpful are Michael D. Clark, *Worldly Theologians* (Washington, D.C.: University Press of America, 1981); James Henry Cotton, *Royce on the Human Self* (Cambridge: Harvard University Press, 1954); John Owen King, *Iron of Melancholy* (Middletown, Conn.: Wesleyan University Press, 1983); Jean Quandt, *From the Small Town to the Great Community* (New Brunswick, N.J.: Rutgers University Press, 1970); Daniel S. Robinson, *Royce and Hocking* (Boston: Christopher, 1968); John K. Roth, ed., *Philosophy of Josiah Royce* (Indianapolis: Hackett, 1982); George Santayana, *Character and Opinion in the United States* (New York: Scribner's, 1924); John E. Smith, *Royce's Social Infinite* (New York: Liberal Arts, 1950); Michael Weinstein, *Wilderness and the City* (Amherst: University of Massachusetts Press, 1982); Raymond Jackson Wilson, *In Quest of Community* (New York: Wiley, 1968); John McDermott, "Josiah Royce's Philosophy of the Community," in *American Philosophy*, ed. Marcus Singer (Cambridge: Cambridge University Press, 1985); and Morton White, *Science and Sentiment in America* (New York: Oxford, 1972). For an overview of changing interpretations, see Walter Conser, "The Reassessment of Josiah Royce," *American Studies* 27 (Fall 1986): 54–60. An important background study is William Goetzmann, ed., *The American Hegelians: An Intellectual Episode in the History of Western America* (New York: Knopf, 1973).

Works on Royce as a Californian are much less frequent. The best are Kevin Starr, *Americans and the California Dream, 1850–1915* (New York: Oxford University Press, 1975), and Earl Pomeroy, "Josiah Royce, Historian in Quest of Community," *Pacific Historical Review* 40 (February 1971): 1–20.

Chapter 1 *("Pioneer Pilgrims")*. The Sarah Royce manuscript on the plains and the gold rush is in BL; the majority of it was published as *A Frontier Lady*, ed. Ralph H. Gabriel (New Haven: Yale University Press, 1932). See also Rodman Paul, "Sarah Eleanor Bayliss Royce," in *Notable American Women*, 3 vols. (Cambridge: Harvard University Press, 1971). The elder Josiah Royce's obituary is useful: Los Gatos *News*, August 24, 1888 (Special Collections, UCLA). The mule incident comes from General Riley's Civil Correspondence, 31st Cong., 1st sess., Sen. Ex. Doc. 52, p. 106. For Martinez, see United States Census, 1852; documents in the trial with Richard C. Swain in the California Historical Society and in the Contra Costa Historical Society, Concord. For the later stops before Grass Valley: Placer County Records, 1–122, BL; Erwin Gudde, *California Gold Camps* (Berkeley: University of California Press, 1975).

Chapters 2–3 *("Grass Valley" and "Avon Farm")*. For Grass Valley the essential sources are in the Searles Historical Library of the Nevada County Historical Society, Nevada City, California. The William Shepard letters proved especially relevant. Issues of early town directories, the Grass Valley *National*, and the *Telegraph* are scattered there, in the Nevada County Public Library, in the Bancroft and the Huntington libraries. Deeds to the Royce properties are in the Nevada County Recorder's Office. See also Frank Oppenheim, "Some New Documents on Royce's Early Experiences of Communities," *Journal of the History of Philosophy* 6 (1968): 381–85. For details of family life and some of the early readings, such as Phineas Camp Headley's *The Miner Boy and His Monitor* (New York: William Appleton, 1864), I am indebted to Nancy A. Hacker.

An essential study is Ralph Mann, *After the Gold Rush: Society in Grass Valley and Nevada City, California, 1849–1870* (Stanford, Calif.: Stanford University Press, 1982). See also Robert Burchell, "Opportunity and the Frontier," *Western Historical Quarterly* 18 (April 1987): 177–96. More descriptive are Jim Morley, *Gold Cities* (Berkeley: Howell-North, 1965), and Robert Wyckoff, *Walking Tours and Twicetold Tales of Grass Valley* (Nevada City, Calif.: Nevada City Publishing Co., 1979). See also E. B. Ware, *History of the Disciples of Christ in California, 1849–1893* (Healdsburg, Calif.: F. W. Cooke, 1916); John Baur, *Growing Up with Califor-*

nia: A History of California's Children (Los Angeles: William Kramer, 1978); and Elliott West, *Growing Up with the Country: Childhood on the Far Western Frontier* (Albuquerque: University of New Mexico Press, 1989).

Josiah's early illness is based on Stephen Royce's Memoirs, RP; the letters of Stephen Royce in Daniel Robinson, *Royce and Hocking: American Idealists* (Boston: Christopher, 1968), 143–56; and Frank Oppenheim's interviews with Marion Royce, 1967, noted in letter to Robert V. Hine, August 17, 1989. Royce's "Miner's Grave," "A Nocturnal Expedition," and "Pussy Blackie's Travels" are in RP.

Chapter 4 *("San Francisco")*. For Josiah's school years in San Francisco, in addition to city histories and directories, see Fannie Cheney's Composition Book, 1869–70, in the California Historical Society Library, San Francisco; Archibald Cloud, *Lowell High School, San Francisco, 1856–1956* (Palo Alto, Calif.: Pacific Books, 1956); "Lincoln School Boys, 1865–1880," Tenth Annual Reunion and Banquet Program, Lincoln Grammar School Association, 1918 (Huntington Library); and *Lincoln Grammar School: A Record Compiled for the Boys* (San Francisco: Lincoln Grammar School Association, 1938), BL. Sam Hall's account of Royce's illness in the shed is in Guy Earl, "Memorabilia," typescript in BL. Myra Daniels's conversation with Nathan Newmark, undated, is in possession of Nancy Hacker. Royce's Intellectual Autobiography (Solomon's, May 27, 1898), in which he describes wandering the streets, is in RP, as is the Autobiographical Note on Influence of Men and Books (RP, vol. 96).

Chapter 5 *("Berkeley Undergraduate")*. For Royce as an undergraduate, see files of the *Berkeleyan*, the *Daily Californian*, the University of California *Register*, Minutes of the Academic Senate, various publications on Class Day and Commencement, the Papers of William Carey Jones and Bernard Moses, and Joseph C. Rowell, "The Beginnings of a Great Library" (MS and typescript, 1938)—all in BL; William W. Ferrier, *Origin and Development of the University of California* (Berkeley: Sather Gate Bookshop, 1930); Verne A. Stadtman, *University of California, 1868–1968* (New York: McGraw-Hill, 1970). For the setting, see city directories and Peter T. Conmy, *Beginnings of Oakland* (Oakland: Oakland Public Library, 1961). For the people he knew, see Alfred R. Ferguson, *Edward Rowland Sill: The Twilight Poet* (The Hague: Martinus Nijhoff, 1955); William B. Parker, *Edward Rowland Sill* (Boston: Houghton Mifflin, 1915); Abraham Flexner, *Daniel Coit Gilman* (New York: Harcourt, Brace, 1946); Fabian Franklin, *Life of Daniel Coit Gilman* (New York: Dodd, Mead, 1910); Joseph Le Conte, *Autobiography*, ed. William D. Armes (New York: Appleton, 1903); Josiah Royce, "Joseph Le Conte," *International Monthly* 4 (1901): 324–34; Lester Stephens, *Joseph Le Conte* (Baton Rouge: Louisiana State University Press, 1982); Benjamin Kurtz, *Charles Mills Gayley* (Berkeley: University of California Press, 1943); Benjamin F. Gilbert, *Pioneers for One Hundred Years: San Jose State College, 1857–1957* (San Jose, Calif.: San Jose State College, 1957); [Ruth Royce], *Historical Sketch of the State Normal School of San Jose,*

California (Sacramento: State Office, 1889). A fellow classmate who wrote about Royce is C. K. Bonestell, "Berkeley in the Seventies," *California Monthly* 43 (Septemeber 1939): 5, 44. Royce recalled his experiences in these years in "The Old and the New—a Lesson," *University [of California] Chronicle* 2 (1902): 92–103.

Chapter 6 *("First Flight")*. The story of the Dorr party is from James Harry Cotton, *Royce on the Human Self* (Cambridge: Harvard University Press, 1954), 4. For the German period, see James M. Hart, *German Universities: A Narrative of Personal Experience* (New York: Putnam's, 1874); Matthew Arnold, *Higher Schools and Universities in Germany* (London: Macmillan, 1874); Clark Spence, *Mining Engineers and the American West* (New Haven: Yale University Press, 1970); and Royce, "Present Ideals of American University Life," *Scribner's* 10 (September 1891): 376–88. The Steffens section is from Justin Kaplan, *Lincoln Steffens* (New York: Simon and Schuster, 1974).

For Johns Hopkins, see Hugh Hawkins, *Pioneer: A History of the Johns Hopkins University, 1874–1889* (Ithaca, N.Y.: Cornell University Press, 1960); John C. Schmidt, *Johns Hopkins: Portrait of a University* (Baltimore: Johns Hopkins University Press, 1986); John C. French, *History of the University Founded by Johns Hopkins* (Baltimore: Johns Hopkins University Press, 1946); Marvin E. Gettleman, ed., *The Johns Hopkins University Seminary of History and Politics*, 5 vols. (New York: Garland, 1987); and the biographies of Gilman above in chapter 5. A copy of Royce's dissertation is in RP.

For the St. Louis Hegelians, consult William Goetzmann, ed., *The American Hegelians: An Intellectual Episode in the History of Western America* (New York: Knopf, 1973); Bruce Kuklick, *Churchmen and Philosophers* (New Haven: Yale University Press, 1985).

Chapter 7 *("Berkeley Exile")*. Many of the references in chapter 5 carry over into these years. The various Royce house addresses can be found in the California Room of the Oakland Public Library. The Bernard Moses Papers are in BL, along with the Minutes of the Academic Senate and the Berkeley Club. Some of the early writings are in Jacob Loewenberg's edition of Royce's *Fugitive Essays* (Cambridge: Harvard University Press, 1925); others, such as the "Thought Diary," are in RP. There are letters and papers of the Head family in BL and now, especially, in the most recently acquired collection of Royce material in the Harvard Archives.

Chapter 8 *("Harvard")*. The Charles Rieber sections are from the Journal of Dorothy Rieber Joralemon, part of it in BL and part in the possession of Peter Joralemon, Gardnerville, Nevada.

For the Harvard years the most useful references have been George Santayana, *Character and Opinion in the United States* (New York: Norton, 1967); Bruce Kuklick, *Churchmen and Philosophers* (New Haven: Yale University Press, 1985) and his *Rise of American Philosophy: Cambridge, Massachusetts, 1869–1930* (New Haven: Yale Unversity Press, 1977); Leroy S. Rouner, *Within Human Experience: The Philosophy of William Ernest*

Hocking (Cambridge: Harvard University Press, 1969); Warren I. Susman, *Culture as History* (New York: Pantheon, 1984); Morton G. White, *Pragmatism and the American Mind* (New York: Oxford University Press, 1973); and Rollo W. Brown, *Harvard Yard in the Golden Age* (New York: Current Books, 1948).
The best commentators on Royce's teaching were Jacob Loewenberg, *Thrice-Born: Selected Memories of an Immigrant* (New York: Hobbs, Dorman, 1968); Harry T. Costello, *Josiah Royce's Seminar, 1913–14* (New Brunswick, N.J.: Rutgers University Press, 1963); Victor Lenzen, Correspondence and Papers, BL; James Mark Baldwin, *Between Two Wars, 1861–1921*, 2 vols. (Boston: Stratford, 1926); John Jay Chapman, "Portrait of Josiah Royce," *Outlook* 122 (July 2, 1919): 372, 377; Charles Bakewell, "Josiah Royce," *Nation* 103 (November 16, 1916): 461–62; Horace Kallen, "Remarks on Royce's Philosophy," *Journal of Philosophy* 53 (February 2, 1956): 131–39; Woodrow Wilson, *Papers*, ed. Arthur Link, (Princeton: Princeton University Press, 1967): 3:10; 18:378. To understand the argument on error, see John E. Smith, "Royce: The Absolute and the Beloved Community Revisited," in *Meaning, Truth, and God*, ed. Leroy S. Rouner (Notre Dame, Ind.: Notre Dame University Press, 1982), 135–53.
For William James, see especially *Letters*, ed. Henry James, 2 vols. (Boston: Atlantic Monthly, 1920); *Selected Unpublished Correspondence, 1885–1910*, ed. F. J. Down Scott (Columbus: Ohio State University Press, 1986); and Ralph Barton Perry, *Thought and Character of William James*, 2 vols. (Boston: Little, Brown, 1935).
For the Australian episode, see Frank Oppenheim, *Royce's Voyage Down Under: A Journey of the Mind* (Lexington: University Press of Kentucky, 1980); Royce, "Reflections after a Wandering Life in Australasia," *Atlantic* 63 (1889): 675–86, 813–28; and Royce, "Impressions of Australia," *Scribner's* 9 (1891): 75–87.
Chapter 9 *("A History and a Novel")*. Two subsequent editions have kept alive Josiah Royce's *California from the Conquest in 1846 to the Second Vigilance Committee in San Francisco: A Study of American Character* (Boston: Houghton Mifflin, 1886). A second edition was published in connection with California's centenary celebration, with an introduction by Robert Glass Cleland (New York: Knopf, 1948); and the most recent edition contains an introduction by Earl Pomeroy (Santa Barbara, Calif.: Peregrine, 1970). Royce's *Feud of Oakfield Creek: A Novel of California Life* (Boston: Houghton Mifflin, 1887) was reprinted, with an introduction by John Clendenning (New York: Johnson Reprint, 1970).
For Scudder, see Ellen Ballou, *Building of the House: Houghton Mifflin's Formative Years* (Boston: Houghton Mifflin, 1970). Reviews of *California* were in *Overland Monthly* 8 (1886): 222–23, 329–30; *Political Science Quarterly* 1 (1886): 491–93; *American Historical Review* 54 (April 1949): 705–6; *Christian Science Monitor*, September 23, 1948, p. 15; *Southern California Historical Quarterly* 30 (September 1948): 249–51; *Mississippi Valley Historical Review* 35 (1948–49): 711–12. For Andrew Rolle, see his

"Exploring an Explorer: Psychohistory and John Charles Frémont,"
Pacific Historical Review 51 (May 1982): 135–63, and *John Charles Frémont:
Character as Destiny* (Norman: University of Oklahoma Press, 1991).
Reviews of *Feud of Oakfield Creek* were in the *Nation* 44 (May 1887): 453;
   Dial 8 (July 1887): 66–68; and *London Quarterly and Holborn Review* 68
   (1887): 384. Compare Walter B. Michaels, *The Gold Standard and the
   Logic of Naturalism* (Berekeley: University of California Press, 1987):
   191–98.
Chapters 10 – 11 *("The West as Metaphysics" and "Retrospect").* The western
   lecture material is from Royce, "The Opening of the Great West, Ore-
   gon, and California," RP, vol. 92. For the professionalization of American
   philosophy see Bruce Kuklick, *Rise of American Philosophy* (New Haven,
   Yale University Press, 1977). In addition to Royce's works, this chapter
   has involved Susan Sontag, *Under the Sign of Saturn* (New York: Farrar,
   Strauss, Giroux, 1980); Raymond J. Wilson, *In Quest of Community*
   (New York: Wiley, 1968); Jean Quandt, *From the Small Town to the Great
   Community* (New Brunswick, N.J.: Rutgers University Press, 1970); Ri-
   chard Robin, *Annotated Catalogue of the Papers of Charles S. Peirce* (Am-
   herst: University of Massachusetts Press, 1967); Thomas Mann, *Doctor
   Faustus* (New York: Knopf, 1948); Horace Kallen, "Remarks on Royce's
   Philosophy," *Journal of Philosophy* 53 (February 1956): 131–39; Michael
   Weinstein, *Wilderness and the City* (Amherst: University of Massachusetts Press, 1982), 36; Clifford Geertz, *Interpretation of Cultures* (New
   York: Basic Books, 1973); William Goetzmann, ed., *American Hegelians*
   (New York, Knopf, 1973); Leroy Rouner, *Within Human Experience:
   the Philosophy of William Ernest Hocking* (Cambridge: Harvard Univer-
   sity Press, 1969); George H. Mead, "The Philosophies of Royce, James,
   and Dewey in their American Setting," *International Journal of Ethics*
   40 (Jan. 1930): 211–31; Patricia Limerick in Donald Worster, et al, "The
   Legacy of Conquest," *Western Historical Quarterly* 20 (August 1989):
   317.
The obituaries cited are in *Daily Californian*, Sept. 18, 1916 (BL); Fresno
   Republican, Dec. 17, 1916; *Pomona College Student Life*, Oct. 9, 1916;
   Anaconda *Standard*, Sept. 24, 1916. For Royce Hall see Ernest Carroll
   Moore, *I Helped Make a University* (Los Angeles: Dawson's, 1952), and
   James Klain, A. J. Band et al, *History of Royce Hall* (Los Angeles: Uni-
   versity of California at Los Angeles, 1985).

Index